Photoshop CS4: Web Design

Student Manual

ACE Edition

Photoshop CS4: Web Design

President & Chief Executive Officer:	Jon Winder
Vice President, Product Development:	Matt Gambino
Vice President, Operations:	Josh Pincus
Director of Publishing Systems Development:	Dan Quackenbush
Writer:	Kirsten Sitnick
Developmental Editor:	Steve English
Copyeditor:	Catherine Oliver
Keytester:	Clifford Coryea

Trademarks

ILT Series is a trademark of Axzo Press.

Some of the product names and company names used in this book have been used for identification purposes only and may be trademarks or registered trademarks of their respective manufacturers and sellers.

Disclaimers

We reserve the right to revise this publication and make changes from time to time in its content without notice.

The Adobe Approved Certification Courseware logo is either a registered trademark or trademark of Adobe Systems Incorporated in the United States and/or other countries. The Adobe Approved Certification Courseware logo is a proprietary trademark of Adobe. All rights reserved.

The ILT Series is independent from ProCert Labs, LLC and Adobe Systems Incorporated, and are not affiliated with ProCert Labs and Adobe in any manner. This publication may assist students to prepare for an Adobe Certified Expert exam, however, neither ProCert Labs nor Adobe warrant that use of this material will ensure success in connection with any exam.

ISBN 10: 1-4260-0525-3
ISBN 13: 978-1-4260-0525-1

Student Manual with data CD
ISBN-10: 1-4260-0527-X
ISBN-13: 978-1-4260-0527-5

Printed in the United States of America

1 2 3 4 5 6 7 8 9 10 GL 11 10 09

Contents

Introduction

After reading this introduction, you will know how to:

A Use ILT Series training manuals in general.

B Use prerequisites, a target student description, course objectives, and a skills inventory to properly set your expectations for the course.

C Re-key this course after class.

Topic A: About the manual

ILT Series philosophy

Our manuals facilitate your learning by providing structured interaction with the software itself. While we provide text to explain difficult concepts, the hands-on activities are the focus of our courses. By paying close attention as your instructor leads you through these activities, you will learn the skills and concepts effectively.

We believe strongly in the instructor-led class. During class, focus on your instructor. Our manuals are designed and written to facilitate your interaction with your instructor, and not to call attention to manuals themselves.

We believe in the basic approach of setting expectations, delivering instruction, and providing summary and review afterwards. For this reason, lessons begin with objectives and end with summaries. We also provide overall course objectives and a course summary to provide both an introduction to and closure on the entire course.

Manual components

The manuals contain these major components:

- Table of contents
- Introduction
- Units
- Appendix
- Course summary
- Quick reference
- Glossary
- Index

Each element is described below.

Table of contents

The table of contents acts as a learning roadmap.

Introduction

The introduction contains information about our training philosophy and our manual components, features, and conventions. It contains target student, prerequisite, objective, and setup information for the specific course.

Units

Units are the largest structural component of the course content. A unit begins with a title page that lists objectives for each major subdivision, or topic, within the unit. Within each topic, conceptual and explanatory information alternates with hands-on activities. Units conclude with a summary comprising one paragraph for each topic, and an independent practice activity that gives you an opportunity to practice the skills you've learned.

The conceptual information takes the form of text paragraphs, exhibits, lists, and tables. The activities are structured in two columns, one telling you what to do, the other providing explanations, descriptions, and graphics.

Appendix

The appendix for this course lists the Adobe Certified Expert (ACE) exam objectives for Photoshop CS4, along with references to corresponding coverage in ILT Series courseware.

Course summary

This section provides a text summary of the entire course. It is useful for providing closure at the end of the course. The course summary also indicates the next course in this series, if there is one, and lists additional resources you might find useful as you continue to learn about the software.

Quick reference

The quick reference is an at-a-glance job aid summarizing some of the more common features of the software.

Glossary

The glossary provides definitions for all of the key terms used in this course.

Index

The index at the end of this manual makes it easy for you to find information about a particular software component, feature, or concept.

Manual conventions

We've tried to keep the number of elements and the types of formatting to a minimum in the manuals. This aids in clarity and makes the manuals more classically elegant looking. But there are some conventions and icons you should know about.

Item	Description
Italic text	In conceptual text, indicates a new term or feature.
Bold text	In unit summaries, indicates a key term or concept. In an independent practice activity, indicates an explicit item that you select, choose, or type.
`Code font`	Indicates code or syntax.

`Longer strings of ▶`
`    code will look ▶`
`    like this.`
	In the hands-on activities, any code that's too long to fit on a single line is divided into segments by one or more continuation characters (▶). This code should be entered as a continuous string of text.

Select **bold item**	In the left column of hands-on activities, bold sans-serif text indicates an explicit item that you select, choose, or type.
Keycaps like (↵ ENTER)	Indicate a key on the keyboard you must press.

Hands-on activities

The hands-on activities are the most important parts of our manuals. They are divided
into two primary columns. The "Here's how" column gives short instructions to you
about what to do. The "Here's why" column provides explanations, graphics, and
clarifications. Here's a sample:

Do it!

A-1:   Creating a commission formula

Here's how	Here's why
1 Open Sales	This is an oversimplified sales compensation worksheet. It shows sales totals, commissions, and incentives for five sales reps.
2 Observe the contents of cell F4	F4 ▼ **=** =E4*C_Rate The commission rate formulas use the name "C_Rate" instead of a value for the commission rate.

For these activities, we have provided a collection of data files designed to help you
learn each skill in a real-world business context. As you work through the activities, you
will modify and update these files. Of course, you might make a mistake and therefore
want to re-key the activity starting from scratch. To make it easy to start over, you will
rename each data file at the end of the first activity in which the file is modified. Our
convention for renaming files is to add the word "My" to the beginning of the file name.
In the above activity, for example, a file called "Sales" is being used for the first time.
At the end of this activity, you would save the file as "My sales," thus leaving the
"Sales" file unchanged. If you make a mistake, you can start over using the original
"Sales" file.

In some activities, however, it might not be practical to rename the data file. If you want
to retry one of these activities, ask your instructor for a fresh copy of the original data
file.

Topic B: Setting your expectations

Properly setting your expectations is essential to your success. This topic will help you do that by providing:

- Prerequisites for this course
- A description of the target student
- A list of the objectives for the course
- A skills assessment for the course

Course prerequisites

Before taking this course, you should be familiar with personal computers and the use of a keyboard and a mouse. Furthermore, this course assumes that you've completed the following courses or have equivalent experience:

- *Photoshop CS4: Basic, ACE Edition*
- *Photoshop CS4: Advanced, ACE Edition*

Target student

The target student for this course is familiar with the basics of using Adobe Photoshop to create and modify digital images. You now want to learn to use Photoshop to prepare consistent, high-quality images and animations for Web use.

Adobe ACE certification

This course is designed to help you pass the Adobe Certified Expert (ACE) exam for Photoshop CS4. For complete certification training, you should complete this course and all of the following:

- *Photoshop CS4: Basic, ACE Edition*
- *Photoshop CS4: Advanced, ACE Edition*
- *Photoshop CS4: Color Printing, ACE Edition*

Course objectives

These overall course objectives will give you an idea about what to expect from the course. It is also possible that they will help you see that this course is not the right one for you. If you think you either lack the prerequisite knowledge or already know most of the subject matter to be covered, you should let your instructor know that you think you are misplaced in the class.

Note: In addition the general objectives listed below, specific ACE exam objectives are listed at the beginning of each topic (where applicable). For a complete mapping of ACE objectives to ILT Series content, see Appendix A.

After completing this course, you will know how to:

- Downsample and trim Web images to decrease file size; use the Save for Web & Devices command to optimize images for Web use; optimize a Web image to a target file size and apply lossy compression to specified image areas; and optimize images with transparency or simulated transparency.

- Create a Web-page layout, and align elements with the grid and Smart Guides; create, edit, and optimize image slices; specify the content type and width of image slices; customize slice names; and export a sliced image as a set of image files with an associated HTML document.

- Use the Slice Options dialog box to specify links and alternate text for slices; use Device Central to create and preview images for mobile devices; and use Zoomify to export high-definition images that can be panned and zoomed.

- Process multiple images in one step; create droplets that perform actions; create HTML-based Web photo galleries; and create multiple variations of a graphic based on variable data.

- Use the Animation and Layers palettes to create animations; and use Photoshop to output animations for use on the Web.

Skills inventory

Use the following form to gauge your skill level entering the class. For each skill listed, rate your familiarity from 1 to 5, with five being the most familiar. *This is not a test.* Rather, it is intended to provide you with an idea of where you're starting from at the beginning of class. If you're wholly unfamiliar with all the skills, you might not be ready for the class. If you think you already understand all of the skills, you might need to move on to the next course in the series. In either case, you should let your instructor know as soon as possible.

Skill	1	2	3	4	5
Downsampling images					
Trimming images					
Optimizing images with the JPEG and GIF formats					
Optimizing an image to a target file size					
Specifying weighted lossy compression					
Creating transparent GIF images					
Choosing matte colors for GIF and JPEG images					
Simulating partially transparent areas					
Creating a Web-page layout					
Laying out a Web page with a grid and Smart Guides					
Creating slices with the Slice tool					
Creating layer-based slices					
Editing slices					
Optimizing slices					
Creating table cells with HTML text					
Naming slices					
Saving HTML and image files					
Assigning links and status-bar messages to slices					
Previewing content for devices					
Exporting an image with Zoomify					
Running the Image Processor script					

Skill	1	2	3	4	5
Creating an action					
Creating a droplet					
Generating a Web photo gallery					
Creating variables for a data-driven graphic					
Creating data sets and exporting a separate file for each data set					
Creating animation frames					
Tweening animation frames					
Blurring to simulate fast motion in an animation					
Exporting animations in Animated GIF format					

Topic C: Re-keying the course

If you have the proper hardware and software, you can re-key this course after class. This section explains what you'll need in order to do so, and how to do it.

Hardware requirements

Your personal computer should have:

- A keyboard and a mouse
- Intel Pentium 4, Intel Centrino, Intel Xeon, or Intel Core Duo (or compatible) processor
- At least 512 MB of RAM
- At least 64 MB of video RAM
- 3.5 GB of available hard disk space (additional free space required during installation)
- A DVD-ROM drive
- Monitor with minimum 1280x960 resolution and 24-bit color or better. (Users of LCD and/or widescreen displays should choose their monitor's native resolution, if possible.)

Software requirements

You will also need the following software:

- Microsoft Windows XP with Service Pack 2 (Service Pack 3 recommended). You can also use Windows Vista Home Premium, Business, Ultimate, or Enterprise with Service Pack 1 (certified for 32-bit editions), but the screen shots in this course were taken in Windows XP, so your screens might look somewhat different.
- Adobe Photoshop CS4 or CS4 Extended.
- Adobe Flash Player.

Network requirements

The following network components and connectivity are also required for rekeying this course:

- Internet access, for the following purposes:
  - Downloading the latest critical updates and service packs from www.windowsupdate.com
  - Downloading the Adobe Flash Player
  - Activating Photoshop CS4
  - Downloading the Student Data files (if necessary)

Setup instructions to re-key the course

Before you re-key the course, you will need to perform the following steps.

1 Download the latest critical updates and service packs from www.windowsupdate.com.

2 From the Control Panel, open the Display Properties dialog box and apply the following settings:

- Theme — Windows XP
- Screen resolution — 1280 by 960 pixels
- Color quality — High (24 bit) or higher

Note: To avoid a blurred or distorted screen, users of flat panel or widescreen displays should either choose their monitor's native resolution, or disable image stretching and scaling if possible. If you choose not to apply these display settings, your screens might not match the screen shots in this manual.

3 If necessary, reset any Photoshop CS4 defaults that you have changed. If you do not wish to reset the defaults, you can still re-key the course, but some activities might not work exactly as documented.

   a While holding Ctrl+Alt+Shift, start Photoshop. This will open a dialog box through which you can return Photoshop to its default configuration.

   b Click Yes to delete the Adobe Photoshop Settings file.

   c Close Photoshop.

4 Configure Photoshop as follows:

   a Start Photoshop.

   b Choose Edit, Preferences, File Handling. Set Maximize PSD and PSB File Compatibility to Always. Click OK.

   c Close Photoshop.

5 If necessary, remove the following droplets from the Windows desktop:

- 150 max width med-high JPEG
- Medium-low JPEG

6 Start Internet Explorer and configure it as follows:

   a Choose Tools, Internet Options. (If you're using Internet Explorer 7, press Alt to show the File menu.)

   b On the General tab, under Home page, click Use blank.

   c On the Advanced tab, under Security, check "Allow active content to run in files on My Computer."

   d Click OK.

   e Close Internet Explorer.

7 If necessary, install the Adobe Flash Player. (Go to www.adobe.com, click the Get Adobe Flash Player button and follow the installation instructions.) You'll need the Flash Player to view Zoomify images in a Web browser, in the unit titled "Web and device features."

8 Create a folder named Student Data at the root of the hard drive. For a standard hard drive setup, this will be C:\Student Data.

9   Download the Student Data files for the course. (If you do not have an Internet connection, you can ask your instructor for a copy of the data files on a disk.)

    a   Connect to www.axzopress.com.

    b   Under Downloads, click Instructor-Led Training.

    c   Browse the subject categories to locate your course. Then click the course title to display a list of available downloads. (You can also access these downloads through our Catalog listings.)

    d   Click the link(s) for downloading the Student Data files, and follow the instructions that appear on your screen.

CertBlaster exam preparation for ACE certification

You can download CertBlaster exam preparation software for ACE certification from our Web site. To do so:

1   Go to www.axzopress.com.

2   Under Downloads, click CertBlaster.

3   Click the link for Photoshop CS4.

4   Save the .EXE file to a folder on your hard drive. (**Note:** If you skip this step, the CertBlaster software will not install correctly.)

5   Click Start and choose Run.

6   Click Browse and navigate to the folder that contains the .EXE file.

7   Select the .EXE file and click Open.

8   Click OK and follow the on-screen instructions. When prompted for the password, enter **c_photocs4**.

Unit 1

Optimizing Web images

Unit time: 60 minutes

Complete this unit, and you'll know how to:

A Downsample and trim Web images to decrease file size.

B Use the Save for Web & Devices command to optimize images for Web use.

C Optimize a Web image to a target file size, and apply lossy compression.

D Optimize images with transparency or simulated transparency.

Topic A: Web image size

This topic covers the following Adobe ACE exam objective for Photoshop CS4.

#	Objective
1.4	Given a scenario, describe the best way to resize an image.
2.6	Explain how to use filters and the Filter Gallery.

Preparing images for the Web

Explanation

When you prepare images for use on a Web site, you should keep their file sizes as small as possible. Smaller images download more quickly for Web users, and this makes your site easier to navigate. If a Web page takes too long to load, visitors might give up and leave your site.

Internet connection speeds and file size

Many home and business users connect to the Internet with a broadband connection. A *broadband* connection is typically any connection that exceeds 56 kbps (kilobits per second), such as a cable, fiber-optic, satellite, or DSL connection. The faster the connection speed, the more quickly Web images download. But many people still connect to the Internet via 56 kbps modems, so you'll have to determine the best balance of image quality and image file size based on your intended audience.

File-size factors

These factors contribute to an image's file size:

Factor	Description
Pixel count	The more pixels in an image, the larger its file size. An image's resolution (number of pixels per inch) has no impact on the file's size or its appearance on the Web—it's the total number of pixels that determines file size and on-screen display size. For example, an image that's 500 pixels wide and tall will appear at the same size on screen whether its resolution is 72ppi or 300ppi. Reducing an image's *pixel dimensions* (width and height in pixels) reduces file size, but also results in a smaller image on screen. To preview an image's size as it will appear in a Web browser, view the image at 100% magnification.
Number of colors	The more colors in an image, the larger its file size. The Save for Web & Devices command can save an image in the GIF format, which specifies a maximum of 256 colors and produces small file sizes. In some cases, however, reducing to 256 colors might destroy image detail, and some colors might be replaced with undesirable colors.
Compression	Most Web images are saved in GIF or JPEG format. The GIF format reduces an image's file size by reducing the number of colors and compressing the image. The GIF format uses *lossless* compression, which compresses the image and preserves the pixel data. The JPEG format uses *lossy* compression, which changes the pixel data and can introduce distortions. The JPEG format supports millions of colors, however, so it's generally best for full-color photographs. In addition, when you use the JPEG format, you can specify a quality setting that balances image quality with file size. You can also use the PNG-8 and PNG-24 formats instead of GIF and JPEG. Although the PNG formats are more robust than GIF and JPEG in some respects, some of their attributes aren't fully supported by older Web browsers.
Additional file information	Some images are saved with additional file information that adds to the file size. For example, an image might be saved with a preview or a color management profile. Fortunately, when you save an image for the Web by using the File, Save for Web & Devices command, all additional file information is stripped from the Web-optimized version of the file.

Do it!

A-1:   Discussing Web image size

Questions and answers

1 Which factor influences an image's file size and Web-browser display size: pixel count or resolution?

2 What other factors influence an image's file size?

3 When you save an image for Web use, how can you strip out additional file data to reduce file size?

Downsampling

Explanation

Web images' file sizes should be as small as possible for faster downloading. It's also best to design a Web page so that site visitors can view entire individual images without having to scroll much. Therefore, you need to consider how well your Web images fit on the page with all the other page elements. You'll often need to reduce image dimensions so that images fit the way you want.

You can use *Hypertext Markup Language (HTML)*—used to create most Web pages— to specify the size at which an image appears. HTML can specify an image's display size but cannot change the actual file size. Therefore, if an image is larger than you want, you should resize it in Photoshop; reducing the image size in Photoshop will also reduce the file size.

When you're starting with an image that is a different size than you want, you can *resample* it to change the number of pixels it contains. You'll typically *downsample* images for the Web, reducing the number of pixels.

To downsample an image:

1 Choose Image, Image Size to open the Image Size dialog box.
2 Check Resample Image to activate the Pixel Dimensions section.
3 Check Constrain Proportions to ensure that the image is resized proportionally.
4 Under Pixel Dimensions, edit the Width and Height values in pixels to specify the dimensions you want the image to have.
5 Click OK.

Web resolution units

When you prepare images for print use, the *resolution* in pixels per inch helps determine the quality of the printed image. For Web images, though, image resolution in pixels per inch isn't a concern, because Photoshop automatically optimizes the resolution when you use the Save for Web & Devices command. The only factor you should consider is the total number of pixels in an image—that is, the image's pixel dimensions.

For example, if you want to ensure that an image will fill half the width of a screen that's 640 by 480 pixels, you'll set its width to about 300 pixels. When the same image is viewed on a monitor set to 1280 by 1024 pixels, the image will fill about one quarter of the monitor's width. Because Web images are measured in pixels, you should use pixels as the measurement unit when working with your images.

Sharpening for the Web

When you downsample an image, Photoshop determines how to assign colors to the new image pixels to best match the appearance of the original image. Photoshop determines this based on the interpolation method you select from a list in the Image Size dialog box. For most images, you should use the default Bicubic method.

No matter which interpolation method you select, the image will often display some blurring after downsampling. You can use the *Unsharp Mask* filter to sharpen an image and restore some of its detail. (The Unsharp Mask filter is a good choice because it offers more control than the simple Sharpen filter does.) For Web images, follow these guidelines:

- In the Unsharp Mask dialog box, use a Radius of 0.3 to 1.0 for most Web images. Don't use 1.5, as you would for print, because you'll get too large a "halo" relative to the details in the image.

- Set the Amount to the value that works best for the image on screen. For print images, you typically make the image a bit over-sharp to get the best results. With images designed for Web use, you should not over-sharpen them; the way they look in Photoshop is the way they will look to a Web audience.

- Typically, a Threshold of zero is good. The Threshold counteracts noise in flat color areas, but with smaller images, noise in flat areas is rarely noticeable, and raising this value can detract from sharpness in small details.

Do it!   ## A-2:   Downsampling images

Here's how	Here's why
1 Start Photoshop	
Open Nutmeg large	From the current unit folder.
	You want to use a smaller version of this image for a Web site.
Save the image as **nutmeg**	When naming images for eventual Web use, you'll generally use all lowercase characters and no spaces.
2 Show the rulers	Press Ctrl+R.
3 Right-click either the horizontal or vertical ruler	To display a shortcut menu, listing the available ruler units.
Choose **Pixels**	To change the ruler units.
4 Choose **Image**, **Image Size...**	To open the Image Size dialog box.
Verify that Constrain Proportions and Resample Image are both checked	
Under Pixel Dimensions, edit the Width box to read **150**	The value in the Height box scales proportionally.
Click **OK**	
5 Choose **Filter, Sharpen, Unsharp Mask...**	To open the Unsharp Mask dialog box.
Lower the Radius value to **0.8**	To avoid a halo around the edges of the image.
Set the Amount value to **90**	
Clear and then check **Preview**	To see how the new settings affect the image. The Unsharp Mask filter makes more of the detail apparent.
Click **OK**	To apply the filter.
6 Update the image	

Trimming

Explanation

Another way to reduce an image's file size is to *trim* (remove) excess pixels from the edge of the image. Many images are bordered by a solid color or by transparency, and you can remove pixels from those areas by using the Trim command.

To trim excess pixels, choose Image, Trim to open the Trim dialog box, shown in Exhibit 1-1. Select options and then click OK.

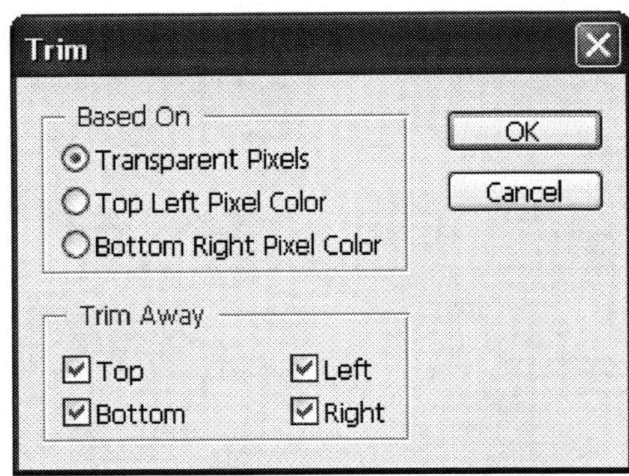

Exhibit 1-1: The Trim dialog box

Do it!

A-3: Trimming images

Here's how	Here's why
1 Expand the image window	(If necessary.) So that you can see the file size information in the status bar.
Observe the file size	`Doc: 57.6K/177.9K` You will trim the image based on the top-left pixel color, which is white. In doing so, you'll also reduce the file size by removing unnecessary portions of the image.
2 Choose **Image, Trim...**	To open the Trim dialog box.
Select **Top Left Pixel Color**	
Under Trim Away, verify that all four options are checked	To trim the areas at the top, bottom, left, and right of the image.
Click **OK**	
3 Observe that not all of the image is trimmed	Some apparent extra white space at the bottom of the image wasn't trimmed because the pixels that make up the soft shadow aren't entirely white.
4 Observe the file size	`Doc: 48.7K/130.0K` (In the status bar.) To see that it's been reduced by trimming the excess areas of the image.
5 Update the image	

Topic B: Optimization

This topic covers the following Adobe ACE exam objectives for Photoshop CS4.

#	Objective
1.2	Describe how to use tabbed documents and the application frame.
12.1	Given a scenario, choose the appropriate Save for Web options for a Web graphic.
12.2	Explain the options in the Save for Web and Devices dialog box.

Optimizing file sizes

Explanation

When you're preparing an image for Web use, you want it to appear with the highest possible quality while having the smallest possible file size. Balancing these two factors to create the best image is called *optimization*. The best way to optimize an image for Web use is to save a copy of the image by using the Save for Web & Devices command. You can use this command to save an image in any of three common Web image formats: JPEG, GIF, and PNG.

In the Save for Web & Devices dialog box, you can use *n*-up (such as 2-up or 4-up) views to compare two or more versions of an image. This will help you choose the best one.

JPEG optimization

The JPEG format is typically used to optimize color photographic images because it supports files with millions of colors. When you save an image in the JPEG format, you can specify a Quality setting, which balances image quality and file size. As you increase the Quality setting, you also increase the file size. The JPEG format uses lossy compression, which alters the image pixel data and removes detail. When the JPEG Quality setting is too low, JPEG compression *artifacts*—irregularities in the image— become visible. You should specify a Quality setting that reduces image file size without producing any visible artifacts.

To save an image in the JPEG format, choose File, Save for Web & Devices to open the Save For Web & Devices dialog box. Although the JPEG format can hold CMYK or Grayscale images as well as RGB images, the Save For Web & Devices dialog box automatically converts images to RGB, as required for display in Web browsers.

To specify JPEG optimization settings, use either of these techniques:

- From the Optimized file format list, select JPEG; then specify the Quality value and other settings.
- From the Preset list, select a JPEG option with preset settings, as shown in Exhibit 1-2.

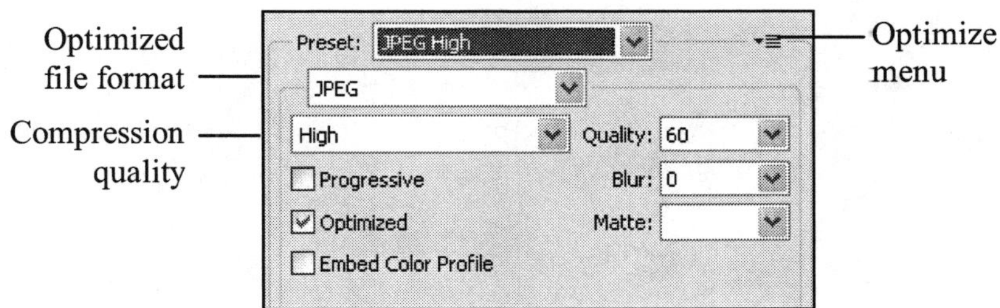

Exhibit 1-2: The JPEG optimization settings in the Save For Web & Devices dialog box

You can specify the following JPEG optimization settings:

Setting	Description
Preset	Applies a JPEG format with preset values. You can create your own JPEG presets by specifying the custom settings you want and choosing Save Settings from the Optimize menu.
Optimized file format	Used when you don't want JPEG presets. Available formats include JPEG, GIF, PNG-8, PNG-24, and WBMP. The format you specify determines the other options that are available for optimizing the image because each format supports different types of settings.
Compression quality	Determines the compression level. You can select a descriptively named compression quality. For example, you can select Very High, which by default specifies a numeric Quality of 80.
Progressive	Creates a progressive JPEG image, which will download in stages so that viewers can see a rough version of the image while the full image is downloading. If you don't check Progressive, the image won't appear at all until it's fully downloaded.
ICC Profile	Retains ICC profile data, which provides color management information that some browsers can use to help ensure that image colors are displayed as you intended. If you want the optimized image to retain its ICC profile data, then check this box. ICC profile data will increase the image's file size, however, and not all Web browsers support this data.
Optimized	Creates an optimized JPEG image, which has a slightly smaller file size but isn't supported by some old Web browsers.
Quality	Used to specify a Quality setting with more precision. You can enter a number in the Quality box or drag the Quality slider.
Blur	Applies a blur to an image to slightly reduce its file size. However, you'll usually get better image quality and a smaller file size by adjusting the Quality setting.
Matte	Used to specify the color you want to use for areas that are transparent in the original image. You should typically specify a Matte color that matches the background color of the Web page on which you'll use the image.
Metadata	Stores information about the image file. You can strip out metadata, or you can include just copyright information, copyright and contact information, all information except data about the camera that created the image, or all metadata.

Do it!

B-1: Optimizing with the JPEG format

Here's how	Here's why
1 Choose **File, Save for Web & Devices...**	To open the Save For Web & Devices dialog box.
Activate the 4-Up tab	To see a preview of the original image, along with three other previews with various optimization settings, so that you can compare them.
2 Verify that the top-right image preview is selected	
From the Preset list, select **JPEG High**	
3 Select the bottom-left preview	
From the Preset list, select **JPEG Medium**	
4 Select the bottom-right preview	
From the Preset list, select **JPEG Low**	
5 Observe the file sizes under each preview	The lower the JPEG quality setting, the smaller the file size.
6 In the Save For Web & Devices dialog box, click 🔍	The Zoom tool.
Click the bottom-right preview twice	To zoom all of the previews to 300% magnification. You can see artifacts around the edges in the JPEG Medium image (with a Quality value of 30), and the effect is even more apparent in the JPEG Low image (with a Quality value of 10).
7 Press (ALT) and click the bottom-right preview twice	To return to 100% magnification. Unless you plan to enlarge the image later, what you see at 100% magnification is what the Web viewer sees. For this image, Medium quality is good enough, producing a file that is a fraction of the original file size with only a small reduction in quality.
	Because you know you won't use the JPEG Low image, you will try some additional settings to see the resulting visual effects and file sizes.
8 Click ✋	To select the Hand tool, so you can click the previews without unintentionally changing the magnification.

9 Verify that the bottom-right
   preview is selected

   From the Preset list, select
   JPEG High

   You'll begin with the presets for JPEG High and
   then modify them.

10 Observe the file sizes for the
   bottom-left and bottom-right
   previews

JPEG		30 quality	JPEG
4.441K			8.44K
2 sec @ 56.6 Kbps			2 sec @ 56.6 Kbps

   You want to see whether you can reduce the file
   size for the bottom-right preview to match that
   of the bottom-left preview by adjusting some of
   the settings.

   Drag the Blur slider to the right

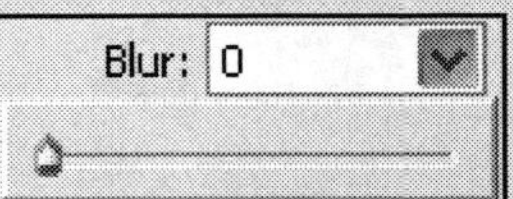

   Release the mouse and observe
   the file size of the bottom-right
   preview

   Drag the Blur slider until the file
   size is approximately 4.4K

   A Blur value of 1.1 will produce a file size of
   4.441K, the same as that of the preview using
   the JPEG Medium preset. Even though the two
   images would have the same file size, the
   bottom-right one is noticeably blurrier.

11 Select the bottom-left preview

   This is the version you will save.

   Click **Save**

   To open the Save Optimized As dialog box.

   Navigate to the current unit folder

   In the Save as type list, verify that
   Images Only (*.jpg) is selected

   Click **Save**

   To save the JPEG-optimized version of the image
   and return to the original Photoshop version.

12 Update and close the image

GIF optimization

Explanation

The GIF format is typically used for images composed of areas of solid colors, such as simple Web graphics or logos. By default, the GIF format doesn't discard any image data, but it does limit image colors to 256. Typically, the fewer colors you use, the smaller the image's file size.

To save an image in the GIF format, choose File, Save for Web & Devices to open the Save For Web & Devices dialog box. To specify GIF optimization settings, do either of the following:

- From the Optimized file format list, select GIF, as shown in Exhibit 1-3. Then specify the GIF settings you want.

- From the Preset list, select a GIF option with preset settings.

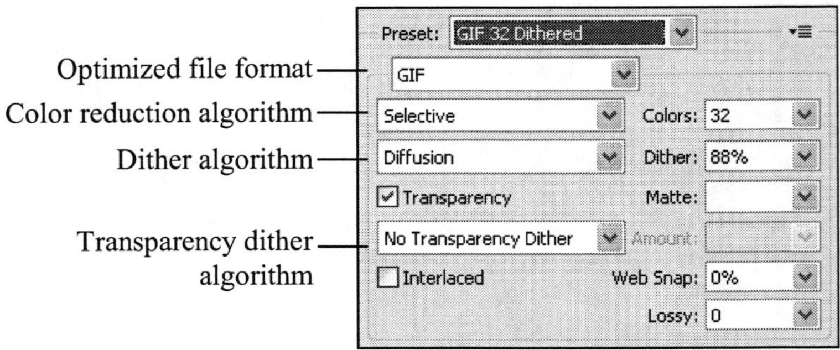

Exhibit 1-3: GIF optimization settings in the Save For Web & Devices dialog box

You can specify the following GIF optimization settings:

Setting	Description
Color reduction algorithm	Specifies fewer colors than the GIF format's maximum of 256. Use this setting to specify the method by which Photoshop determines which colors the optimized image should use. The colors are listed in the Color Table.
Dither algorithm	Determines the dithering method used (if any): Diffusion, Pattern, or Noise. *Dithering* is a technique that creates the illusion of additional colors (or shades of gray) by varying the pattern of dots or pixels. When an image's colors are reduced, Photoshop can simulate a color that no longer exists by filling that area with a pattern of pixels of two or more similar colors in the panel. The area then appears to be filled with a solid color similar to the original color.
Transparency	Used to include transparent areas in the optimized GIF image. Unlike the JPEG format, the GIF format supports transparency. GIF supports only areas of full transparency or full opacity, however, so it can't display partial transparency.
Transparency dither algorithm	Specifies the method for dithering partially transparent areas. The GIF format can't display partially transparent pixels, but you can simulate the effect by applying a transparency dither to replace partially transparent pixels with a pattern of solid and transparent pixels.
Amount	Specifies how much transparency dithering to use.
Interlaced	Specifies that the GIF image will appear in stages as it's downloaded, rather than not appearing at all until fully downloaded.
Lossy	Discards some image data to reduce file size.
Colors	Specifies the number of colors used in the image.
Dither	Specifies the amount of dithering used in the image. A higher dithering value simulates more colors and is useful for making gradients appear smoother. Increasing the Dither value might increase the file size.
Matte	Specifies a matte color in areas that are transparent in the original image.
Web Snap	Specifies how close a color must be to a Web-safe color before it will be converted to a Web-safe color. *Web-safe colors* are the 216 colors that are the same on both Macintosh and Windows computers when only 256 colors are available. However, many Internet users today use monitors that display thousands or millions of colors, making this option less relevant.

Do it!

B-2: Optimizing with the GIF format

Here's how	Here's why
1 Open Logo on gradient	From the current unit folder.
2 Choose **File, Save for Web & Devices...**	To open the Save For Web & Devices dialog box. Because the 4-Up tab was active when you last viewed this dialog box, that tab is still active.
Observe the second image preview	It uses 32 colors and an 88% dither.
Observe the bottom image preview	It uses 32 colors but no dither. The gradient in the bottom image preview has more noticeable vertical banding than does the gradient in the second image preview.
3 Select the second image preview	If necessary.
Drag the Dither slider to **100%**	To smooth out the vertical banding. The file size has increased somewhat, which is why the default value might be a good choice.
4 From the Colors list, select **8**	To see how decreasing the number of colors affects the image's appearance and file size.
In the Colors list, type **9**	To increase the number of colors by one.
Continue increasing the number of colors while observing the edges of the text	The text edges look gritty until there are about 13 colors in the image.
5 Compare the 13-color, 100% dither preview (the second one) with the 16-color, 88% dither preview (the third one)	The second preview has only a slightly larger file size, but the gradient looks smoother overall.

6	Select the second image preview	If necessary.
	Click **Save**	To open the Save Optimized As dialog box.
	Edit the File name box to read **logo**	
	Click **Save**	
7	Update and close the image	Even though you didn't edit the image itself, you are prompted to save changes because Photoshop remembers the Save For Web & Devices settings.
8	Open Recipes page title	(From the current unit folder.) Sometimes when you need to reduce the file size substantially, it might be better not to use dithering at all.
9	Open the Save For Web & Devices dialog box	Choose File, Save for Web & Devices.
	Select the top-right image preview	If necessary.
	Set the Colors value to **8**	This image preview uses an 88% dither.
	For the bottom-right image preview, set the Colors value to **8**	This image preview uses no dither.
		The drop shadows on both previews look somewhat banded, so this setting is less than ideal. You might need to use it, though, if the entire page produces too large a file size.
		The vertical and horizontal elements in the "R" and "e" look chipped in the dithered version, but they don't in the non-dithered one.
10	Save the bottom-right version as **recipestitle**	
	Update and close the image	

Topic C: Fine-tuning quality

This topic covers the following Adobe ACE exam objectives for Photoshop CS4.

#	Objective
12.1	Given a scenario, choose the appropriate Save for Web options for a Web graphic.
12.2	Explain the options in the Save for Web and Devices dialog box.

Comparing options

Explanation

When you're optimizing an image for Web use, the choice of file format is not always obvious. You can use the previews in the Save For Web & Devices dialog box to compare optimization options for an image by specifying different file formats and settings. You can use additional options to help determine which file format and settings will work best for your image.

To determine the best optimization settings for an image, you can use the Save For Web & Devices dialog box to specify settings for one preview, and then instruct Photoshop to automatically apply alternate settings to the other two previews for comparison. For example, you can specify particular JPEG settings for one preview and then choose Repopulate Views from the Optimize menu. The remaining previews will display the image in the same file format but with different settings.

Optimize to File Size

You might want to optimize an image in order to use a specific file size—for example, to match the file sizes of other images on a Web page. If you know the target file size for a particular image, you can instruct Photoshop to determine the best settings to use to achieve that target file size.

To optimize an image to a specified file size:

1. Open the Save For Web & Devices dialog box.
2. From the Optimize menu, choose Optimize to File Size to open the Optimize To File Size dialog box. (This command optimizes images for only the GIF and JPEG formats.)
3. In the Desired File Size box, enter the target file size.
4. Under Start With, if the selected preview uses GIF or JPEG and you want to use the current format, select Current Settings. If you want Photoshop to select the best format to use to meet the target size, select Auto Select GIF/JPEG.
5. Click OK.

Do it!

C-1: Optimizing to a target file size

Here's how	Here's why
1 Open Logo on canvas	In the current unit folder.
2 Open the Save For Web & Devices dialog box	

3 For the second image preview, from the Preset list, select **JPEG High**

You'll begin with high JPEG quality to avoid artifacts. Note that this image has a photographic element, and it's often better to use JPEG for mixed photographic and flat-color images.

Because of the photographic portion of the image, the 256-color limit in GIF images might not give you the results you want. Also, its non-lossy compression is less efficient for creating smaller files with photographic material.

4 From the Optimize menu, choose **Repopulate Views**

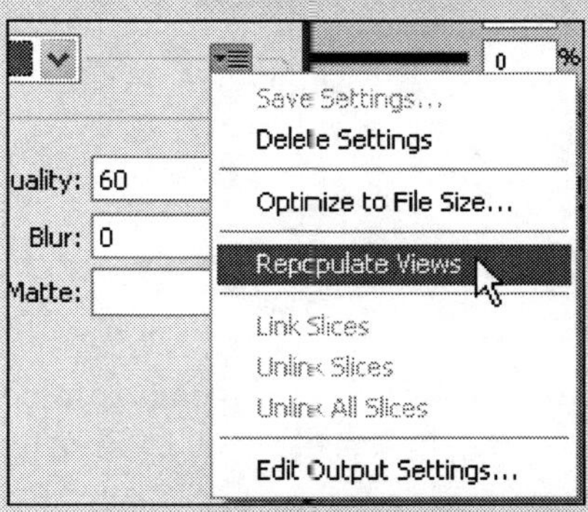

(The button for the Optimize menu is to the right of the Preset list.) To create additional JPEG image previews with Quality values of 30 and 15.

5 From the Zoom Level list, select **200%**

(In the bottom-left corner of the dialog box.) The artifacts on the characters are noticeable, particularly in the bottom two previews. The third preview (with the Quality value of 30) is the best compromise between image quality and file size. However, you want this image's file size to match that of another, similar image on your Web page.

6 Select the third preview

From the Optimize menu, choose **Optimize to File Size...**

To open the Optimize to File Size dialog box.

Edit the Desired File Size box to read **12**

Select **Auto Select GIF/JPEG**

You'll let Photoshop determine the best file type for the image.

Click **OK**

Photoshop sets the Quality value to 22, with JPEG as the file type.

7 Save the optimized image as **logo-on-canvas**

Changing lossiness

Explanation

In the Save For Web & Devices dialog box, you can further reduce a GIF-optimized image's file size by using the Lossy setting. The default Lossy value is zero, which means that no lossy compression is applied. Increasing the Lossy value decreases the file size but introduces image distortions. These distortions are particularly noticeable in solid-color areas and in text.

Do it!

C-2: Changing lossiness

Here's how	Here's why
1 Open the Save For Web & Devices dialog box	For the Logo on canvas image.
2 Select the second image preview	(If necessary.) The image quality is good, but you'll experiment to see whether you can get better results with the GIF format.
From the Optimized file format list, select **GIF**	The default Colors setting is 8, but this is inadequate for the image of the peppers.
From the Colors list, select **32**	Now the peppers are red again.
3 Drag the Lossy slider up to **100**	This value produces noise on the text, but the background is usable. This setting also drops the file size quite a bit—almost one-third of the original size.
Experiment with different Lossy values	
Drag the Lossy slider back to **0**	
Click **Cancel**	To close the dialog box.
4 Close all images, updating as necessary	

Topic D: Creating transparency

This topic covers the following Adobe ACE exam objectives for Photoshop CS4.

#	Objective
12.1	Given a scenario, choose the appropriate Save for Web options for a Web graphic.
12.2	Explain the options in the Save for Web and Devices dialog box.

Formats that support transparency

Explanation

If an image contains transparent areas that you want the Web-optimized version to include, you must select a Web image format that supports transparency.

The GIF, PNG-8, and PNG-24 formats all support transparency. However, the GIF and PNG-8 formats can't display partial transparency—pixels are displayed as either fully transparent or fully opaque. Both formats can apply dithering to simulate partial transparency. (The JPEG format doesn't support transparency at all.) The JPEG 2000 format, an optional Photoshop plug-in, does support transparency. For you to view JPEG 2000 image files on the Web, however, your browser must have a JPEG 2000 plug-in.

To display true partial transparency, you can use the PNG-24 format. The newest Web browsers can display PNG-24 images, but some older browsers can't display multilevel transparency in PNG-24 images. For example, Netscape 6 and higher and Mozilla Firefox 1 and later support multilevel PNG transparency, but Internet Explorer 6 for Windows does not. Safari and Firefox for Macintosh both support multilevel PNG transparency.

Do it!

D-1:   Creating transparent GIF images

Here's how	Here's why
1 Open nutmeg	In Photoshop format, from the current unit folder.
Hide the Shadow and Color Fill 1 layers	Note that the nutmeg image has transparency around it.
2 Open the Save For Web & Devices dialog box	Because the JPEG format doesn't support transparency, you will use a GIF format.
3 Verify that the top-right preview is selected	
From the Preset list, select **GIF 32 Dithered**	The preview shows the transparent areas.
4 Clear **Transparency**	To put a white background into the image. When you don't want transparency in an image that has it, you can place a white background in it.
Check **Transparency**	To remove the white background, restoring the transparent areas.
5 Save the selected preview as **nutmeg-default-trans**	In the current unit folder.

Matte colors

Explanation

When you're optimizing a GIF image that includes transparency, a harsh edge might appear where the opaque pixels border the transparent area. To prevent this, you can apply a matte color to any semitransparent pixels in the original image. If the matte color matches the Web page's background color, it will soften the transition between the opaque pixels and the transparent areas.

Similarly, when optimizing a JPEG image that originally includes transparency, you can specify a matte color to fill all transparent areas. The matte color should match the Web page's background color so that the areas that were transparent in the original image will seem to be transparent in the optimized version.

Hexadecimal colors

Computer monitors use red, green, and blue to make all colors you see, and a hexadecimal scheme is used to identify different combinations of those colors: the first two characters represent the intensity of red, the next two of green, and the last two of blue. Hex notation uses the scale 0123456789ADCDEF, with 0 representing almost no color and F representing 15 times the intensity of 0.

Hexadecimal characters can be a combination of letters and numbers. When creating a Web page in HTML, you can use hexadecimal values to specify colors for Web page components. For example, you can use hexadecimal values in the HTML code to specify background colors for Web pages and table cells.

Because the HTML code identifies certain colors by their hexadecimal values, you can exactly match a matte color to a Web page's background color by specifying the same hexadecimal value. To specify a matte color in the Save For Web & Devices dialog box:

1   Click the Matte box to open the Choose a color dialog box.
2   Edit the # box to specify the color's hexadecimal code.
3   Click OK.

A computer monitor uses light to display color. When you add the colors together, you get white; the absence of all colors is black (as if you've turned the light off). So, for example, 000000 (the lowest level of red, green, and blue) is black, and FFFFFF—or #FFFFFF—is white. To get yellow, you would add red and green, but no blue, so the hex code would be FFFF00.

Do it! **D-2: Choosing matte colors for GIF and JPEG images**

Here's how	Here's why
1 Start Internet Explorer	
Choose **File, Open...**	Or press Ctrl+O.
Browse to the current unit folder	
Open transparency-GIF-default	This HTML page displays the image file you just created with three different background colors so you can see possible unattractive edges.
	The image looks good on white, passable on light yellow, but bad on dark blue, because the image was on a white matte in Photoshop by default. In addition, a white speck appears at the top-right of the image when it's on a dark background. This area wasn't pure white, so it didn't get converted to transparency earlier.
2 Close Internet Explorer	
Return to Photoshop	If you know the image will be on a dark background, you can save it with that color for a matte. Doing this will affect colors that were semitransparent in the original image, tinting the resulting color with the matte.
3 Open the Save For Web & Devices dialog box	For the nutmeg image.
Click the Matte color swatch, as shown	
	To open the Color Picker dialog box.
Edit the # box to read **000099**	This is the hexadecimal value of the dark blue color.
Click **OK**	To return to the Save For Web & Devices dialog box.
4 Save the top-right image preview as **nutmeg-dark-matte**	

5 In Internet Explorer, open transparency-GIF-dark-matte

(From the current unit folder.) This time, you see a dark-blue fringe in the first two images, but the image looks just right on the dark blue background.

Return to Photoshop

Next, you'll experiment with the JPEG format. If an image will be placed on a solid background, you can use JPEG, but you should choose the correct matte color.

6 Open the Save For Web & Devices dialog box

From the Preset list, select **JPEG High**

Set the Matte color to **000099**

Click the Matte swatch to open the Choose a color dialog box. Edit the # box and click OK.

The blue color appears in the entire background because JPEG doesn't support transparency.

Save the image as **nutmeg-dark-bkgd**

7 In Internet Explorer, open transparency-JPEG-dark-bkgd

(From the current unit folder.) The only area of the image that looks good is the solid background that uses the matching matte color.

Return to Photoshop

Close Internet Explorer.

Partial transparency

Explanation

When an original image includes partial transparency, you can optimize it for the Web by using the PNG-24 file format. Partial transparency will be maintained in the optimized image, but not all Web browsers support partial transparency. Another option is to save the image in the JPEG format and apply a matte color that matches the Web page's background color.

If the Web page's background isn't a single solid color, the most effective technique is to optimize the image in the GIF or PNG-8 file format, with which you can specify a transparency dither. From the Transparency dither algorithm list, select a dithering option; then specify a matte color that will look acceptable over multiple backgrounds. The transparency dither will create a pattern of transparent pixels and matte-colored pixels to simulate partial transparency. The areas of the image that were fully transparent will remain fully transparent in the optimized version.

Do it!   ## D-3: Simulating partially transparent areas

Here's how	Here's why
1 Show the Shadow layer	Keep the Color Fill 1 layer hidden. The shadow is created by using areas of partial transparency.
2 Open the Save For Web & Devices dialog box	
From the Preset list, select **GIF 32 Dithered**	
Save the image as **nutmeg-with-shadow**	In the current unit folder.
3 In Internet Explorer, open transparency-GIF-with-shadow	(From the current unit folder.) The image looks good on a solid white background, but the extra white around the shadow is obvious against the other backgrounds.
Return to Photoshop	
4 Open the Save For Web & Devices dialog box	
From the Preset list, select **PNG-24**	
Save the image as **nutmeg-24-bit-trans**	
5 In Internet Explorer, open transparency-PNG	(From the current unit folder.)

If you're using Internet Explorer 7, the image is displayed properly on all of the solid backgrounds. However, if you're using Internet Explorer 6, the image isn't displayed properly because IE6 for Windows doesn't support PNG transparency.

Return to Photoshop

6 Open the Save For Web &
Devices dialog box

From the Preset list, select
GIF 32 Dithered

From the Transparency dither
algorithm list, select **Diffusion
Transparency Dither**

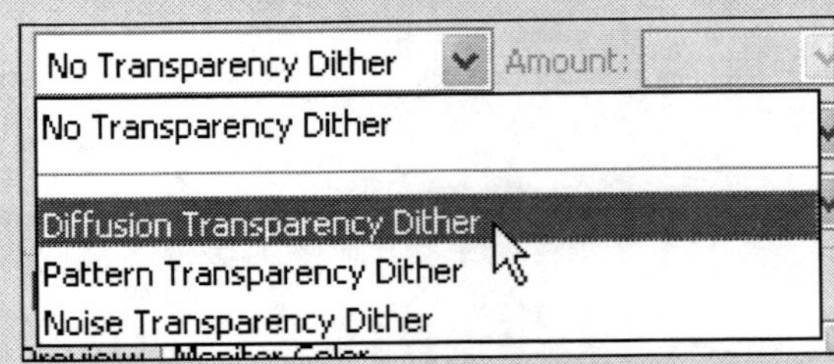

To create a dithered pattern where there was
originally partial transparency. The pixels will
still appear either completely solid or
transparent, but the alternating pattern of solid
and transparent color will simulate the partial
transparency as effectively as possible given the
GIF format's limitations.

7 Click the Matte color swatch

To open the Color Picker dialog box.

Edit the # box to read **808080**

This time, you're choosing a middle-gray matte
color that will look acceptable on both white and
a darker color, rather than one that will look
good on one color and bad on the other.

Click **OK**

To return to the Save For Web & Devices dialog
box.

Save the image as
nutmeg-diffusion-trans

In the current unit folder.

8 In Internet Explorer, open
transparency-GIF-diffusion

(From the current unit folder). Observe the
dithered pattern. The result isn't as pleasing as
the real shadow, but the dithered pattern still
suggests a shadow.

Return to Photoshop

9 Update and close the image

Unit summary: Optimizing Web images

Topic A   In this topic, you learned about factors that influence **image file size**. In addition, you used the Image Size command to **downsample** images for Web use. Finally, you used the **Trim** command to remove excess pixels from image borders.

Topic B   In this topic, you used the Save for Web & Devices command to **optimize** an image in the JPEG and GIF formats for Web use.

Topic C   In this topic, you used the **Repopulate Views** command to generate additional previews with varying settings based on the selected preview. In addition, you instructed Photoshop to specify optimization settings automatically to achieve a **target file size**. Finally, you applied a **lossiness** setting to specified areas of an image, while masking other areas from the lossy compression.

Topic D   In this topic, you learned about the Web-optimized formats that support **transparency**, and you learned about Web browsers that support **partial transparency**. In addition, you learned how to select **matte colors** for GIF and JPEG images to smoothly blend opaque pixels with transparency or with a Web page's background color.

Independent practice activity

In this activity, you'll prepare an image for Web use by resampling, sharpening, trimming, and optimizing it. You'll optimize the image in several formats, using various settings.

1 Open Cumin large. Save the image as **My cumin large** in Photoshop format.

2 Resample the image to 120 pixels wide.

3 Sharpen the image.

4 Trim the image to remove the excess white areas.

5 Optimize the image for the Web with the file name **cumin** in a medium JPEG format.

6 View the image in Internet Explorer. (*Hint*: In the Windows Internet Explorer dialog box, display the Files of type list and select JPEG Files. Select cumin and click Open.)

7 Return to Photoshop and hide the Color Fill 1 layer.

8 Optimize the image for the Web as a GIF file with transparency. (*Hint*: Select GIF 32 Dithered. From the Transparency dither algorithm list, select Diffusion Transparency Dither.) Save the optimized image as **cumin-trans**.

9 View the image in Internet Explorer.

10 Close Internet Explorer.

11 Update and close all images.

Review questions

1 You're using the Save For Web & Devices dialog box to prepare an image for Web use by specifying the JPEG format. Which color mode will the image use?

  A Grayscale

  B CMYK Color

  C RGB Color

  D Indexed Color

2 Why is the Unsharp Mask filter often better than the simple Sharpen filter?

  A The Unsharp Mask filter is not subject to pixelation the way the Sharpen filter is.

  B The Sharpen filter can produce a dull border around the image.

  C The Unsharp Mask filter offers a greater degree of control than does the Sharpen filter.

  D The Sharpen filter can over-sharpen an image.

3 Name three factors that contribute to an image's file size.

4 True or false? It's important to save Web images at a resolution of no more than 96 ppi.

5 You can use the __________ command to eliminate excess pixels, such as transparent or white space, from the edges of an image.

6 In the Save for Web & Devices dialog box, you can use __________ views to compare two or more versions of an image.

7 When you're placing photographic images on a Web site, which format is generally the best to use so that you get a good balance of image quality and file size, and ensure widespread browser compatibility?

  A GIF

  B JPEG

  C TIFF

  D PNG

8 When you're placing illustrations with flat color areas on a Web site, which format is generally the best to use if you want widespread browser compatibility?

  A GIF

  B JPEG

  C TIFF

  D PNG

9 If you have a desired target file size for an image, what command should you choose from the Optimize menu in the Save For Web & Devices dialog box?

10 Which formats support transparency, even if not all browsers can display it properly? [Choose all that apply.]

A GIF

B JPEG

C TIFF

D PNG

11 How can you simulate transparency in a JPEG image that will appear on the Web?

A Use the Opacity slider in the Layers panel.

B Specify a Matte color in the Save For Web & Devices dialog box.

C Check Transparency in the Save For Web & Devices dialog box.

D Check Interlaced in the Save For Web & Devices dialog box.

12 If you want to make an image with transparency appear without light edges on a dark background, you should specify a dark ______ color in the Save For Web & Devices dialog box.

13 True or false? You can create images with semi-transparent pixels that can be displayed properly in all browsers in widespread use.

Unit 2

Slicing images

Unit time: 75 minutes

Complete this unit, and you'll know how to:

A Create a Web-page layout, and align elements with the grid and Smart Guides.

B Create, edit, and optimize image slices.

C Specify the content type and width of image slices.

D Customize slice names, and export a sliced image as a set of image files with an associated HTML document.

Topic A: Full-page designs

This topic covers the following Adobe ACE exam objective for Photoshop CS4.

#	Objective
12.5	Explain how to create a sliced Web image.

Image slices

Explanation

When you're designing a Web page with many image elements, it's often best to create the page as a single image. You can then *slice* the image into several smaller graphics to make up the Web page. The advantages of this approach include the following:

- Although the Web page is composed of several images and other elements, they fit together seamlessly because they were created from a single sliced image.

- When you're creating a Web-site navigation bar (or *navbar*), it's much easier to create it as a single image sliced into its components, rather than to create each component as a separate file in Photoshop.

- When you divide a single image into slices, it seems to download quickly because individual slices begin to appear, instead of users having to wait until the entire image downloads.

Although Photoshop can prepare images effectively for the Web, as well as apply some HTML formatting, it's best to use Photoshop in conjunction with a dedicated Web authoring program such as Dreamweaver. With Photoshop, you can optimize images for Web use, and with a Web authoring program, you can arrange the images with other page content, such as text, video, and tables.

Page design

When you're designing a Web page, you should ensure that it will work reasonably well with a variety of monitor sizes and resolutions. For example, specify a page width that will fit even fairly small monitors so your viewers won't have to scroll horizontally to see content that's cut off. The page width you choose will depend partly on your intended audience.

Most people accessing the Internet today (with desktop or laptop computers) use monitor resolutions of at least 800×600 pixels. Because a Web browser might not occupy the entire screen width, and because the browser's components will occupy part of the screen, a target width of about 750 pixels should ensure that most of your site's visitors will be able to view the entire page width.

Do it!   **A-1: Creating a Web-page layout**

Here's how	Here's why
1 Press D	(If necessary.) To set the foreground and background colors to the defaults.
2 Choose **File, New...**	To open the New dialog box.
3 Edit the Name box to read **roughdesign**	
4 From the Preset list, select **Web**	The default size is 640×480 pixels. You'll enter a custom image size that's typical of the width of a full-page design.
5 Edit the Width box to read **750**	Observe that the Size box is now dimmed.
6 Edit the Height box to read **400**	
7 From the Background Contents list, select **White**	If necessary.
8 Click **OK**	To create the image file.

Positioning and aligning items

Explanation

When you design an image for Web use, you can position and align items accurately by using a visible grid. In addition, you can use *Smart Guides*—nonprinting guide lines that appear automatically—to align items with other items and locations.

To display and customize the grid:

1   Choose View, Show, Grid to display the grid.
2   Choose Edit, Preferences, Guides, Grid, Slices & Count to open the Preferences dialog box with the Guides, Grid, Slices & Count settings showing.
3   Edit the "Gridline every" box to specify where horizontal and vertical guidelines will appear, and select a unit of measure from the list.
4   Edit the Subdivisions box to specify additional guidelines that will appear between the gridlines.
5   Click OK.

When moving items, you can use the following techniques:

- To drag an item, use the Move tool.
- To create a duplicate, press Alt as you drag an item.
- To constrain the movement to horizontal, vertical, or a 45° angle, press Shift as you drag an item.
- To enable or disable Smart Guides, choose View, Show, Smart Guides. When Smart Guides are enabled, they appear automatically as you drag an item so that you can easily align it.

Do it!   **A-2:   Laying out a Web page with a grid and Smart Guides**

Here's how	Here's why
1 Choose **View**, **Show**, **Grid**	To display a grid over the entire image. You'll change the grid size.
2 Choose **Edit**, **Preferences**, **Guides, Grid, & Slices...**	To open the Preferences dialog box with the Guides, Grid, Slices & Count settings displayed.
Edit the Gridline every box to read **100**	
From the list, select **pixels**	Gridline every: 100 pixels Subdivisions: 4
Edit the Subdivisions box to read **10**	To create additional gridlines every 10 pixels.
Click **OK**	To apply the new settings and close the dialog box. Next, you'll block out some areas where you want a navigation bar (navbar) and colored panels to appear.
3 In the toolbox, click and hold	(The Rectangle tool.) To display the list of related tools.
Select the **Rounded Rectangle Tool**	
Draw a rectangle in the area indicated	As you draw the shape, the tool snaps to the gridlines.
4 Create a second rounded rectangle, as shown	

5 Select the Move tool

Press ⟨ALT⟩ and begin dragging the second rectangle to the right

To duplicate the rectangle you just drew.

While pressing ⟨ALT⟩, press ⟨SHIFT⟩ and continue to drag

To constrain the movement horizontally as you drag.

When the duplicate rectangle is in position, as shown, release the mouse button; then release ⟨ALT⟩ + ⟨SHIFT⟩

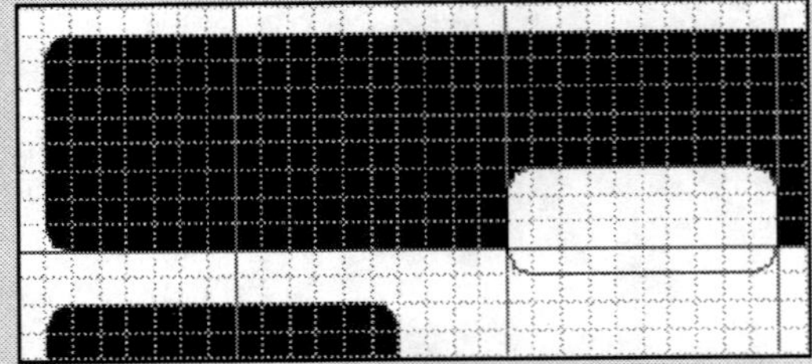

6 Press ⟨X⟩

To switch the foreground and background colors.

7 Drag to create a tab that is 100 pixels wide and 40 pixels tall and that overlaps the top rectangle, as shown

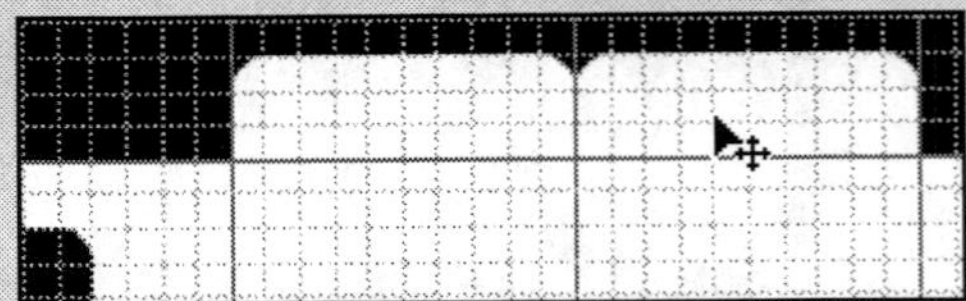

(Using the Rounded Rectangle tool.) To create a shape that you'll use as a tab on a navbar.

8 Select the Move tool

Press ⟨ALT⟩ and drag the rectangle to the right, as shown

To duplicate the tab you just created.

9 Select the Type tool

   In the Control panel, set the type
   to **Arial**, **16 pt**

   Press (D)   To use the default foreground and background
               colors.

   Click inside the left tab you
   created, as shown, and type
   Products

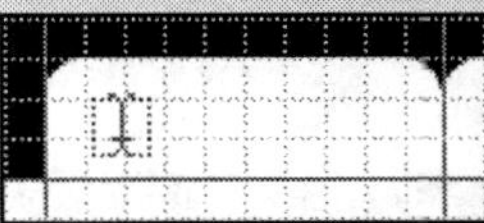

   Press (↵ ENTER) on the numeric
   keypad

   To complete the edit.

10 In the second tab, type **Recipes**,
   aligned with the bottom of the tab,
   as shown

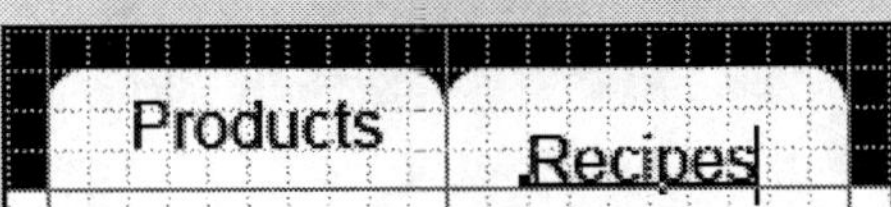

   (Remember to press Enter on the numeric
   keypad after you've entered the text.) You'll use
   Smart Guides to align "Recipes" and
   "Products."

11 Choose **View**, **Show**, **Grid**   To hide the grid so you can see the effect of
                                          Smart Guides.

   Choose **View**, **Show**,   To enable Smart Guides.
   Smart Guides

12 Using the Move tool, drag the   To observe the Smart Guides.
   Recipes label

   Press (SHIFT) and drag the Recipes
   label to align it with the Products
   label, as shown

   Use the Smart Guides.

13 Save the image in Photoshop   In the current unit folder.
   format as **roughdesign**

14 Choose **View**, **Show**,   To hide Smart Guides.
   Smart Guides

   Close the image

Topic B: Basic slicing

This topic covers the following Adobe ACE exam objective for Photoshop CS4.

#	Objective
12.5	Explain how to create a sliced Web image.

Slicing techniques and types

Explanation

You can divide a Web image into rectangular slices and then optimize and customize them in ways not possible with a single image. For example, you can specify a different URL link for each slice. Or you might have a large image that contains a small portion with a drop shadow. You can slice the image and then use the Save For Web & Devices dialog box to optimize the slice with the shadow in a format that supports transparency.

When you save a sliced image, each slice is saved as a separate file in a folder named "images," within the folder you specify. In addition, an HTML file is generated to display the set of sliced images as one seamless image, with each slice in a table cell.

You can create slices by using a variety of techniques. The technique used to generate a slice determines its type and its functionality. An icon called a *badge* appears on each slice to identify its type or to provide other information. The following table describes the types of slices and their uses.

Slice type	Badge icon	Description
User	(image content) (no image content)	Created with the Slice tool or the Slices From Guides command. You can optimize user slices individually. You can also promote an auto or layer-based slice to a user slice. User slices display a solid border and a blue badge to differentiate them from auto slices.
Auto		Generated automatically to fill gaps between the user slices or layer-based slices you create, because the entire image must be filled with slices. Auto slices display a dotted border and a gray badge with a link icon. All auto slices in an image are linked, indicating that they share the same optimization settings.
Layer-based		Created from layers. A *layer-based slice* includes all of the pixels from the layer. The slice is moved and resized as you move and modify the layer content. For that reason, layer-based slices are useful for navbar buttons and other sliced areas that you might want to rearrange or alter. In addition, if you apply a layer style, such as a drop shadow, to the layer content, the layer slice enlarges to accommodate it.
Subslices		A type of auto slice that is created where slices intersect.

When you export a sliced image, the individual graphic file generated for each slice is given the same name as the original image, with a number corresponding to its slice number. Therefore, it's useful to give the original image the same name as the Web page for clarity.

Do it!

B-1:   Creating slices with the Slice tool

Here's how	Here's why
1 Open index	From the current unit folder.
Save it as **my_index**	
Choose **View, Fit on Screen**	
2 In the toolbox, select	(The Slice tool is in the Crop tool group.) To activate the Slice tool options in the Control panel.
3 In the Control panel, click **Slices From Guides**	Using this option makes all slices user slices. This can be inconvenient. If you move user slices, they might end up overlapping or creating a gap, thereby generating additional slices.
Choose **Edit, Undo Slices From Guides**	
4 Show the grid	Choose View, Show, Grid.
Choose **View, Snap To** and verify that Grid is checked	
5 Using the Slice tool, drag a slice around the logo, as shown	
Observe the new slice	The slice you just created is labeled 03. All of the other slices surrounding it are auto slices. If you moved the slice you created, the auto slices would adjust; this is more convenient than if all of the slices were user slices.
6 Create a vertical slice between the logo and tabs, as shown	

7 Create a slice around the Search
   box and the Go button, as shown

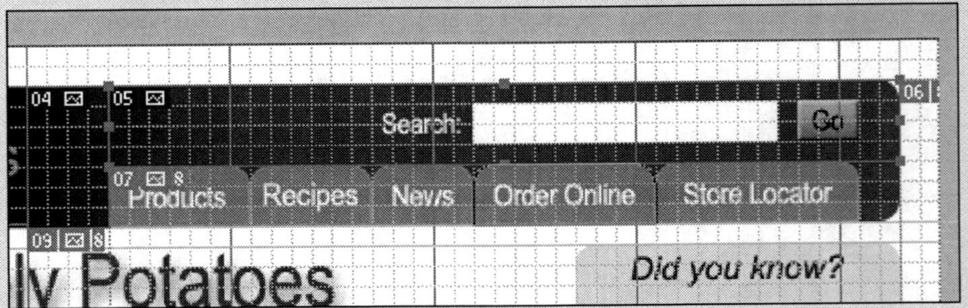

Start above the first tab, adjacent to the slice you just created, and snap to the gridline at the top edge of the tabs. Be sure to include the two grid squares to the right of "Go."

8 Create slices around the left and
   right colored panels, as shown

The "Nutmeg" and "Did you know?" panels.

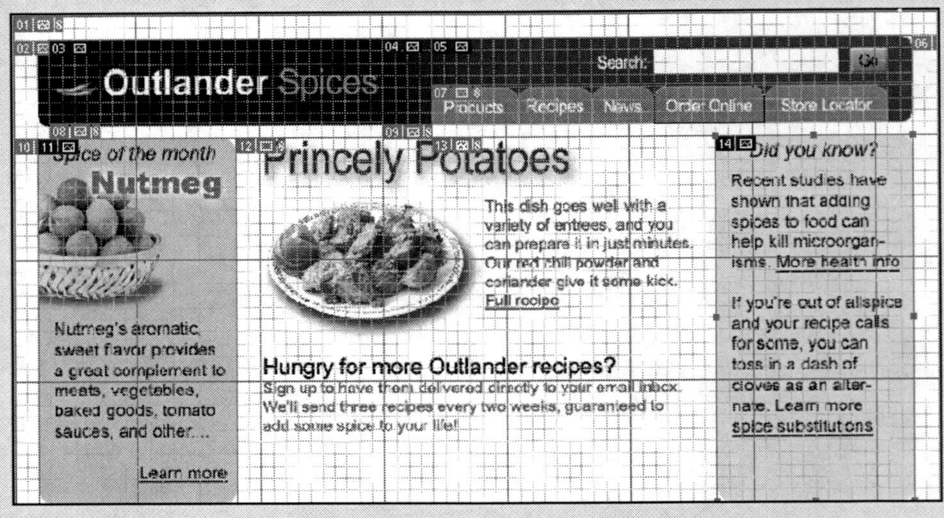

9 Update the image

Layer-based slices

Explanation

If particular image regions are already divided among several layers, you can generate slices by converting each layer to an individual slice. Layer-based slices are useful for content that you might want to move or modify, because as you move or resize the layer content, the associated layer-based slice is moved or resized along with it.

To create slices based on layers, select the layers in the Layers panel and then choose Layer, New Layer Based Slices. You can use the Move tool to move the layer content, and the associated layer-based slice will move with it.

Do it!

B-2:   Creating layer-based slices

Here's how	Here's why
1 Drag the left edge of the Layers panel to the left	So you can read the full names of the text layers.
Select the Products tab layer	
Press (SHIFT) and click the Store Locator tab layer	To select the tab layers.
2 Choose **Layer, New Layer Based Slices**	
Observe the badges for the layer-based slices	

08 Products 09 Recipes 10 News 11 Order Online 12 Store Locator

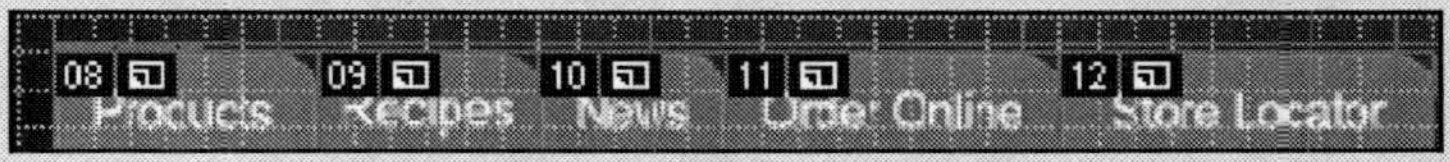	
	These badges are different from those of the user slices. Note also that the slices that follow have been renumbered.
3 Select the Move tool	You'll be moving Store Locator to the left of Order Online.
In the Layers panel, select the Order Online tab layer	
In the image, drag the Order Online tab to below the words "add some spice" in the white area	

some spice to your life! 23 Order Online 24 25

(Anywhere in the blank space at the bottom center of the image, under the text, will do.) The slice moves with the layer, and the slice number is updated.

4　Select the Store Locator tab layer

Drag to place it to the right of the News tab, as shown

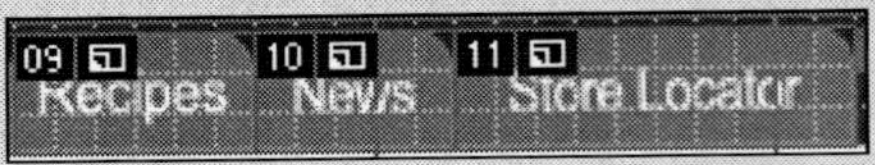

5　Select the Order Online tab layer

Drag to position it as shown

6　Press (CTRL) + (H)

To hide all of the "extras" so that you can see the image without gridlines, guides, or slices.

Press (CTRL) + (H)

To view the extras.

7　Update the image

Slice editing

Explanation

You can move and resize user slices by using the Slice Select tool.

- To move a user slice, point inside it and drag.
- To resize a user slice, click it to select it, point to one of the selection handles on the slice's edge, and then drag.
- To convert a user slice to an auto slice, select it with the Slice Select tool and press Delete.

When you resize or move a user slice, it snaps to the objects selected in the View, Snap To submenu if it gets within four pixels of an object, such as a gridline or another slice. If you drag a slice close to another slice but leave a gap between them, auto slices are generated to fill the gap. Snapping slices to the grid and to other slices can help you avoid generating auto slices.

Overlapping slices

When you move or resize a slice, it might overlap other slices. To change the stacking order of slices, first select the slice you want to rearrange; then, in the Control panel, click a button as shown in Exhibit 2-1 to move the slice in the stacking order.

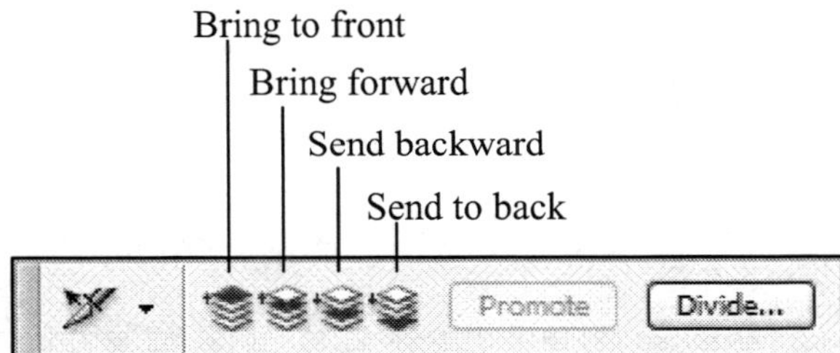

Exhibit 2-1: Stacking-order buttons for slices

B-3: Editing slices

Here's how	Here's why
1 In the toolbox, click and hold 	To show the related tools.
Select the **Slice Select Tool**	
2 Select slice 04	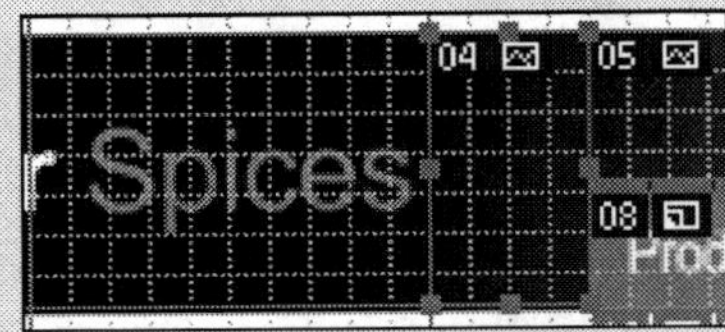
	(The slice dividing the logo from the navbar in the title bar.) A border appears around the slice when you select it.
Choose **Select, Deselect Layers**	So that no layers are selected. If a layer were selected, you might delete the layer's contents, rather than the slice you've selected.
Press (DELETE)	This still leaves an auto slice. Now you'll see what happens if you overlap slices.
3 Select slice 03	The slice that contains the logo.
Drag the right handle of slice 03 so that it overlaps the user slice to its right by one minor grid square	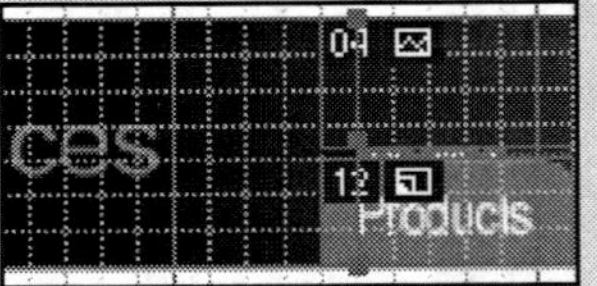
	Slice 05 becomes slice 04. Photoshop still considers the boundary of slice 04 to be its original position, because that slice is higher in the stacking order.
4 Verify that slice 03 is selected	
In the Control panel, click 	(The Bring forward button.) The actual boundary that will appear between slices 03 and 04 in the HTML table is now determined by the edge of slice 03 because it's now higher in the stacking order.
	Additionally, Photoshop splits slice 03, adding a slice below it because of slice 03's intersection with the Products tab slice.
	You'll now examine another potential problem.

5 Choose **View**, **Snap To**, **None**

So that slices won't snap to objects when you move or resize them.

Drag the right handle of slice 03 toward the left, more than one minor gridline, as shown

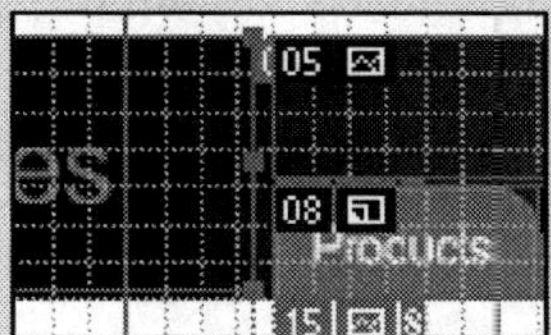

Photoshop creates an auto slice 04 in the gap between slices 03 and 05, but it's so small it's difficult to see. When you don't use the Snap To option, Photoshop often creates auto slices, generating extra small graphics unnecessarily.

6 Choose **Edit**, **Undo Resize Slices**

7 Choose **View**, **Snap To**, **All**

8 Drag the right handle of slice 03 to the left

Until it snaps to the minor gridline along the left edge of the Products tab.

9 Update the image

Optimizing sliced images

Explanation

One of the benefits of slicing a Web image is that you can optimize each slice individually. All auto slices generated in a sliced image, however, share the same optimization settings. You can select any auto slice to specify the optimization settings for all of the auto slices. To specify optimization settings for individual slices, open the Save For Web & Devices dialog box and use the Slice Select tool to select a slice; then specify the settings you want to use.

Previewing optimized slices

In the Save For Web & Devices dialog box, the file size for the preview image reflects the size of the slice you've selected. To see the file size for the entire image, press Ctrl+A to select all of the slices.

You might want to apply the same optimization settings to several slices. To do so, in the Save For Web & Devices dialog box, press Shift and click the slices you want to select. Then apply the desired settings.

Linking slices

You can link slices so that they share optimization settings. In addition to simplifying changes, linking slices also aligns dither patterns between adjacent linked slices. This is mainly noticeable for GIF images with very few colors.

To link slices:

1   In the Save For Web & Devices dialog box, use the Slice Select tool to select a slice.
2   Press Shift and click each additional slice you want to include in the linked set.
3   From the Optimize menu, choose Link Slices.
4   Select any of the linked slices to specify optimization settings that will apply to the entire linked set.

Do it!   ## B-4:   Optimizing slices

Here's how	Here's why
1 Open the Save For Web & Devices dialog box	
2 At the bottom of the dialog box, click as shown	
	To display the Select Browser Menu.
Choose **Edit List...**	To open the Browsers dialog box.
3 Click **Add**	To open the Preview In Other Browser dialog box.
Navigate to the Program Files folder and select **iexplore**	The Internet Explorer executable file is typically located in C:\Program Files\Internet Explorer.
Click **Open**	To add Internet Explorer to the Browsers list.
4 Select **iexplore**	In the Browsers dialog box.
Click **Set As Default**	If necessary.
Click **OK**	To close the dialog box.
5 Next to the Select Browser Menu, click	To preview the image in Internet Explorer.
Close Internet Explorer	
6 Activate the Optimized tab	To see only one view of the image.
Press ⟮SHIFT⟯ and click each slice	To select all of the slices. Use the Hand tool to scroll the image.
From the Preset list, select **GIF 32 Dithered**	This is a good overall setting for most of this image, which has a lot of flat color. You'll change the setting for individual slices later. This image already includes guides that you can use to generate slices.
7 On the left side of the dialog box, click	(The Toggles Slices Visibility button.) To hide the slices temporarily so that you can more easily see the image. The photo of the potatoes would look better if it were in JPEG format.
Press ⟮Q⟯	To show the slices.

8 Press (ALT) and click
   Remember

   Release (ALT) and click **Done**

   To keep the settings you've specified.

   To close the dialog box.

9 Using the Slice tool, create a slice
   with the edges snapped to the
   gridlines, as shown

You'll specify optimization settings for this slice
that are different from those for the rest of the
image.

10 Create a slice around the word
    "Nutmeg" and the nutmeg photo,
    as shown

The slice should extend to the edge of the text
above and below "Nutmeg" and the photo, and
to the left and right edges of the panel.

11 Open the Save For Web &
    Devices dialog box

    Select the slice containing the
    image of the Princely Potatoes
    dish

    Observe the file size for the slice

    (Below the image.) You'll see whether changing
    the settings increases or decreases the slice's
    size.

    From the Preset list, select
    JPEG Medium

    The appearance of the food and the shadow
    improve, while the file size for the slice has
    actually decreased.

12 Optimize the nutmeg slice so that
    it uses the **JPEG Medium** preset

    The image quality improves for the selected
    slice, and its file size decreases.

13 Click the slice containing the
Outlander Spices logo

The gradient at the top appears banded
(distinctly visible vertical stripes appear instead
of a smooth color transition). You want it to
look smoother. The gradient is split across two
slices.

Press (SHIFT) and click slice 04

To select both slices.

From the Optimize menu, choose
Link Slices

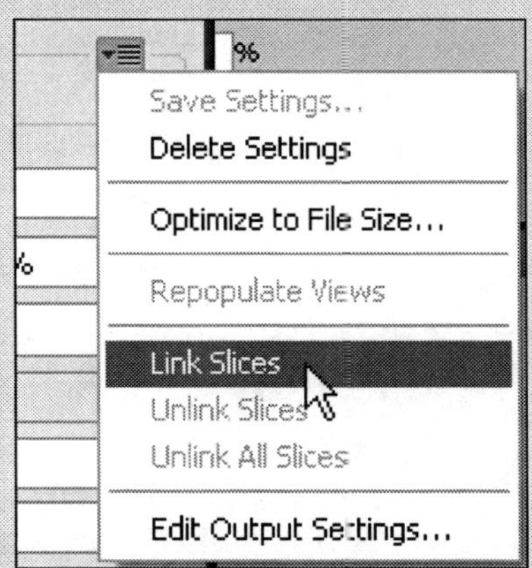

14 Press (Q)

To hide the slices.

From the Preset list, select
GIF 128 Dithered

The banding in the gradient is lessened in both
slices, and the file size increases slightly.

15 Click **Done**

16 Update the image

Topic C: Advanced slicing

This topic covers the following Adobe ACE exam objective for Photoshop CS4.

#	Objective
12.5	Explain how to create a sliced Web image.

Image text and HTML text

Explanation

In addition to optimizing individual slices, you can specify that some slices display HTML text instead of image data.

Changing image text to HTML text

If you're creating Web content based on a sliced image, you might want to replace most of the text from the image with HTML text. Some slices might contain text, but by default, it will be stored as image data, which requires more storage space than HTML text. In addition, site visitors won't be able to search for text that's saved as image data. Finally, if you use HTML text, you can use HTML tags to format it.

To specify that text in the original image should be HTML text instead of image data:

1   Create or select a slice containing image text.
2   Open the Save For Web & Devices dialog box.
3   Double-click the slice to open the Slice Options dialog box, shown in Exhibit 2-2.
4   Verify that Text is HTML is checked.
5   From the Slice Type list, select No Image.
6   In the Text Displayed in Cell box, enter the desired text and HTML tags.
7   Click OK.

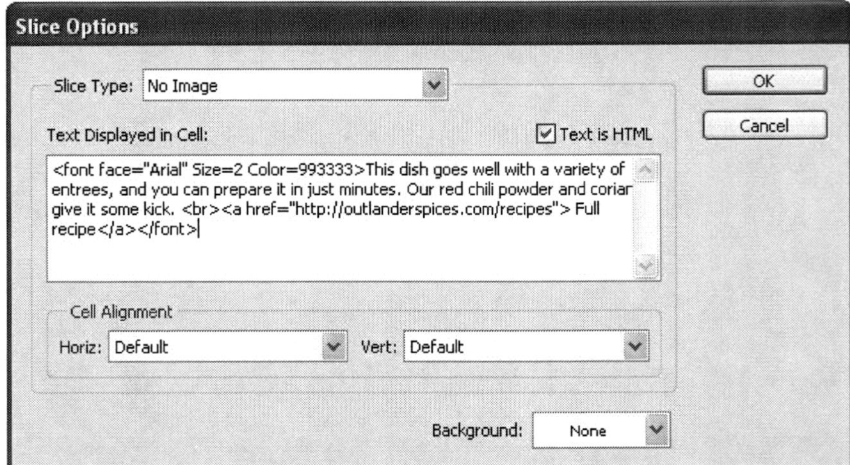

Exhibit 2-2: The Slice Options dialog box

HTML formatting

When you want to format text with HTML tags, you add a tag before the text you want to format. At the end of the text, you add a closing tag. The closing tag is typically the same as the opening tag but is preceded by a "/" character—for example, `<strong>` and `</strong>`.

Although you can apply some basic HTML text formatting directly in Photoshop, you should apply most text formatting by using Cascading Style Sheets (CSS) in an HTML editing application, such as Dreamweaver. In that application, you'd open and edit the HTML file you exported from Photoshop.

The following table lists a few basic HTML tags you can use to format HTML text in Photoshop.

HTML tag	Description
`<strong>`	Displays the text with a stronger emphasis than the text around it, usually by applying bold formatting.
`<b>`	Makes text bold.
`<i>`	Makes text italic.
`<font face = "font name" size = x>`	Specifies the typeface and size for the text, where x indicates the type size. The type size is specified as a value from 1–7. These values aren't points or pixels but are based on the default text size specified by each viewer's Web browser. A value of 3 is the same as the default text size in the viewer's browser, with sizes 1–2 representing smaller text sizes, and 4–7 representing larger sizes.
`<p>`	Indicates a paragraph break.
` `	Indicates a line break.

If you want to insert a link, the HTML code is a bit more complicated. It consists of the anchor tag, `<a>`, followed by the `<href>` tag, which includes the URL of the link. For example, the HTML code for a link might appear as follows:

```
<a href="http://outlanderspices.com">Outlander Spices</a>
```

You can find lists of HTML tags online by searching for "HTML tags" with an Internet search engine.

Do it!

C-1: Creating table cells with HTML text

Here's how	Here's why
1 Open the Save For Web & Devices dialog box	
Click	To preview the image in Internet Explorer.
Select any of the text on the page	You can't, because the text is an image. Internet users, however, usually expect text on a Web site to be selectable, because they might want to copy and paste it into another program.
Close Internet Explorer	To return to Photoshop.
Click **Done**	To close the Save For Web & Devices dialog box.
2 Using the Slice tool, create a slice as shown	
3 Using the Type tool, click anywhere in the text	To activate the type layer.
Press CTRL + A	To select all of the text.
Press CTRL + C	To copy the text.
4 Using the Slice Select tool, right-click the slice	To display the shortcut menu.
Choose **Edit Slice Options...**	To open the Slice Options dialog box.
5 From the Slice Type list, select **No Image**	
Click in the Text Displayed in Cell box	
Press CTRL + V	To paste the text you copied.
Click **OK**	To close the dialog box. The slice's badge now indicates that it's a non-image slice.
6 Open the Save For Web & Devices dialog box	

7	Double-click the slice containing the text	To open the Slice Options dialog box. It contains the text you pasted into it, but Web-specific options are also available.
	Verify that Text is HTML is checked	
	Add tags to the text, as shown	

```
<font face="Arial" Size=2 Color=993333>This dish goes well with a variety of
entrees, and you can prepare it in just minutes. Our red chili powder and coriar
give it some kick. <br><a href="http://outlanderspices.com/recipes"> Full
recipe</a></font>
```

		To format the text similar to the way it's formatted in Photoshop.
	Click **OK**	To close the dialog box.
8	Preview the image in Internet Explorer	
	Drag across the text you converted to a No Image slice	You can select this text because it's not an image.
	Close Internet Explorer	To return to Photoshop.
	Click **Done**	To close the Save For Web & Devices dialog box.
9	Update the image	

Topic D: Exporting Web pages

This topic covers the following Adobe ACE exam objective for Photoshop CS4.

#	Objective
12.1	Given a scenario, choose the appropriate Save for Web options for a Web graphic.
12.2	Explain the options in the Save for Web and Devices dialog box.
12.5	Explain how to create a sliced Web image.

Exporting slices

Explanation

When you're finished optimizing and modifying image slices, you can export them as individual graphics with an associated HTML file. You can then open the exported HTML file in an HTML editing application, such as Dreamweaver, to further prepare the page for use on the Web. Before you export the sliced image, you can name the graphics that will be generated from it.

Named slices

By default, an image file generated from a slice is given the original image name, followed by an underscore and the slice name, which might be a number or a layer name. It can be useful to customize the names for some exported images so you'll be able to identify them more easily. For example, it's more likely that you and others would know the purpose of an image named navbar_logo.gif than of an image named index_07.gif.

In addition, when you're creating multiple Web pages that will contain a particular image, you can store a single copy of that image on the Web server and have each page refer to that image. This will save space on the Web server because you're storing only one copy of the image, instead of a separate copy for each page on which it's used. In addition, the site will download more quickly because the image will be downloaded only once. Because multiple pages will refer to a particular image file, you should not precede its file name with a particular Web page's document name.

Slices that you've specified as No Image will be exported as HTML, not as images. To customize an image slice name, right-click it and choose Edit Slice Options. In the Slice Options dialog box, edit the Name box as desired. Or, with the Slice Select tool selected, click the Slice Options button in the Control panel.

Do it!   **D-1:   Naming slices**

Here's how	Here's why
1 Select the slice containing the logo	You'll name the navbar items so they're not specific to this document and thus can be used more easily by other Web pages.
Right-click the slice and choose **Edit Slice Options...**	To open the Slice Options dialog box.
Edit the Name box to read **navbar_logo**	
Click **OK**	To close the dialog box.
2 Right-click the slice containing the Products tab and choose **Edit Slice Options...**	
Edit the Name box to read **products_tab**	
Click **OK**	
3 Rename each of the other slices containing tabs to reflect the text on the tab	Rename the slices containing the text Recipes, News, Store Locator, and Order Online. For example, you would rename the slice containing the Recipes text as recipes_tab. You might rename the last two tabs as store_tab and order_tab.
4 Name the slice to the right of the navbar **navbar_right**	
5 Name the slice containing the Search box **navbar_search**	
6 Update the image	

Exporting sliced images with HTML

Explanation

After preparing a sliced image, you'll need to export it for further editing in an HTML editor or for use on the Web. You can export each slice as a separate image file along with an HTML document to display the images, or you can export only the images or only the HTML file.

To export a sliced image:

1   Choose File, Save For Web & Devices.
2   Click Save to open the Save Optimized As dialog box.
3   From the Save as type list, select the components you want to export:
   - HTML and Images (*.html)
   - Images Only (*.gif)
   - HTML Only (*.html)
4   In the File name box, enter a name for the HTML file.
5   From the Slices list, select the category of slices you want to export.
6   Click Save.

The images are stored in an automatically generated folder named "images." The images folder and the HTML document are stored in the location you specified in the Save Optimized As dialog box.

Do it!   ## D-2:   Saving HTML and image files

Here's how	Here's why
1 Open the Save For Web & Devices dialog box	You've already sliced the image as desired and specified all of the optimization settings. Now you'll export the image for use on the Web or for further editing in an HTML editor.
2 Click **Save**	To open the Save Optimized As dialog box.
3 In the Save in list, navigate to the current unit folder	
From the Save as type list, select **HTML and Images (*.html)**	
Edit the File name box to read **index.html**	This is the typical file name used for the index or home page of a Web site.
Use the default settings	With the default settings, all slices will be exported, along with the associated HTML file.
Click **Save**	
4 In Internet Explorer, open index.html	From the current unit folder.
5 Close Internet Explorer	
6 In Windows Explorer, navigate to the current unit folder	
Double-click the **images** folder	To see that Photoshop has saved each slice individually.
7 In Photoshop, hide gridlines and slices	
Update and close the my_index image	

Unit summary: Slicing images

Topic A In this topic, you created a **Web-page layout**. You displayed a customized **grid** and aligned items with it. Finally, you moved and duplicated items and used **Smart Guides** to align items with one another.

Topic B In this topic, you used the Slice tool to create **user slices**. You also created **layer-based slices**. In addition, you used the Slice Select tool to move and resize slices. Finally, you optimized individual slices and **linked slices**.

Topic C In this topic, you set slices to display **HTML text** instead of image data.

Topic D In this topic, you customized slice names and **exported** a sliced image as a set of image files with an associated HTML document.

Independent practice activity

In this activity, you'll create layer-based slices and additional user slices. You'll format text as HTML text, and export a sliced image.

1 Open gallery. Save the image as **my_gallery** in the current unit folder.

2 Create slices from the navbar button layers. (*Hint*: Show the slices. In the Layers panel's Navbar set, select from the Products tab to the Store Locator tab, and choose Layer, New Layer Based Slices.)

3 Create additional user slices similar to those shown in Exhibit 2-3. (*Hint*: Show the grid. The numbering of the slices in your image might differ from those shown in the exhibit.)

4 Format the text on the right, below the "Did you know?" heading, as HTML text. (*Hint*: First, copy the text. Then use the Save For Web & Devices dialog box. Replace the paragraph-break characters in the text with <p> tags.)

5 Preview the image in Internet Explorer. Close Internet Explorer.

6 Export the image to generate the individual graphics and HTML files needed to display the material on the Web.

7 Hide gridlines and slices.

8 Update and close the image.

9 Open my_gallery.html in Internet Explorer to preview the exported materials. Then close Internet Explorer.

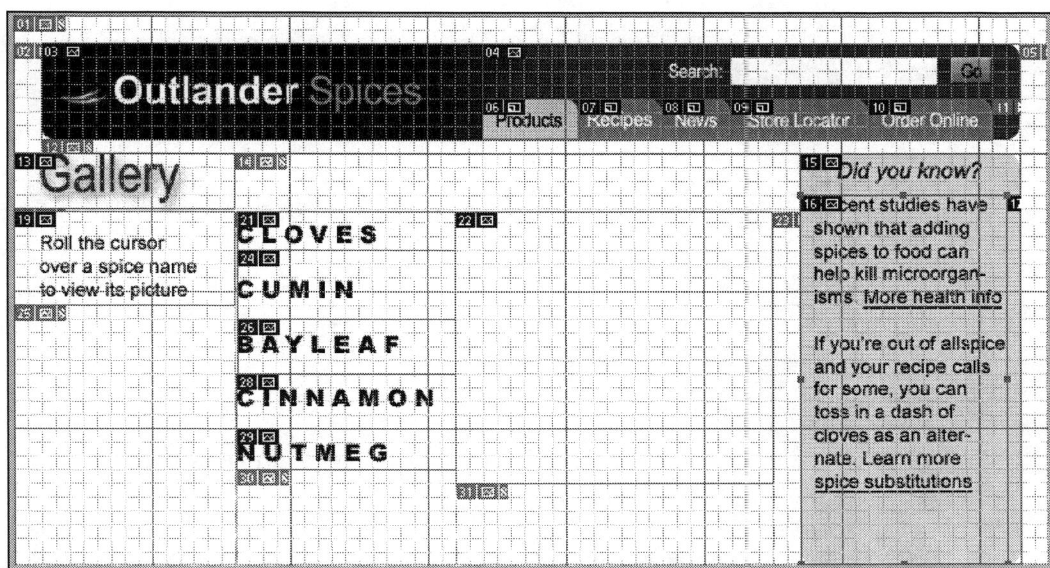

Exhibit 2-3: The image slices as they appear after Step 3 of the independent practice activity

Review questions

1 True or false? It's good practice to keep a Web-page design to fewer than 800 pixels wide.

2 Slices that you create with the Slice tool are called __________ slices.

3 True or false? You can create slices that overlap one another.

4 Why might you use slices to optimize an image for Web use? [Choose all that apply.]

   A To specify different optimization settings for different parts of an image.

   B To create a navigation bar from a single image.

   C To ensure that the image won't appear in a Web browser until it is completely downloaded.

   D To maintain the image layers in the Web version of the image.

5 To make slices share optimization settings, you can:

   A Group them.

   B Put them in a slice set.

   C Link them.

   D Merge them.

6 You can designate that a slice contain: [Choose all that apply.]

   A An image

   B Plain text

   C HTML text

   D A sound

7 What do you use to control the named slices when they're exported?

   A The Slice Settings dialog box

   B The Save For Web & Devices dialog box

   C The Slice panel

   D The Slice Options dialog box

8 You want to export a sliced image for use on the Web. Which of the following can Photoshop output?

   A Only the HTML file

   B Only the slices

   C A single JPEG, GIF, or PNG image

   D The slices, the HTML, or both

Unit 3

Web and device features

Unit time: 50 minutes

Complete this unit, and you'll know how to:

A Use the Slice Options dialog box to specify links and alternate text for slices.

B Use Device Central to create and preview images for mobile devices.

C Use Zoomify to export high-definition images that can be panned and zoomed.

Topic A: Links and status-bar messages

This topic covers the following Adobe ACE exam objective for Photoshop CS4.

#	Objective
12.5	Explain how to create a sliced Web image.

Explanation

One of the benefits of slicing an image in Photoshop is that you can assign a different URL to each slice. In a Web-page image that includes areas you want to define as buttons, you can define each button area as a slice and then assign a URL to each slice.

Links and Alt text

To specify a link for a slice, right-click it and choose Edit Slice Options. Then, in the URL box (in the Slice Options dialog box), enter the Web address for the link.

Links can have different target frames. A link's *target* specifies whether the link opens in the current browser window or in a new browser window. In the Slice Options dialog box, in the Target box, you can enter code to specify where the link will open:

- Enter **_blank** to open the link in a new browser window. The original window will remain open.
- Enter **_self** to open the link in the original window, replacing the page currently being viewed.
- Enter **_parent** to open the link in a new parent frameset. For example, if your Web page uses frames, and the current frame is a child, then specifying the link's target as _parent will open it in the current parent frame.
- Enter **_top** to have the link replace all current frames in the original window.

Also, you can enter text in the Message Text box. Typically, when a user points to a link, its URL appears in the browser's status bar. If you enter text in the Message Text box, however, that text will appear instead. For example, you can enter "Click here for more information"; when a user points to the link, that message will appear in the status bar.

Finally, you can specify alternate text for any slice by entering text in the Alt Tag box, as shown in Exhibit 3-1. The alternate text appears in place of the image when viewed in a browser that doesn't show images. The alternate text also appears while the image is loading, and most browsers display the alternate text as a tooltip or in the status bar.

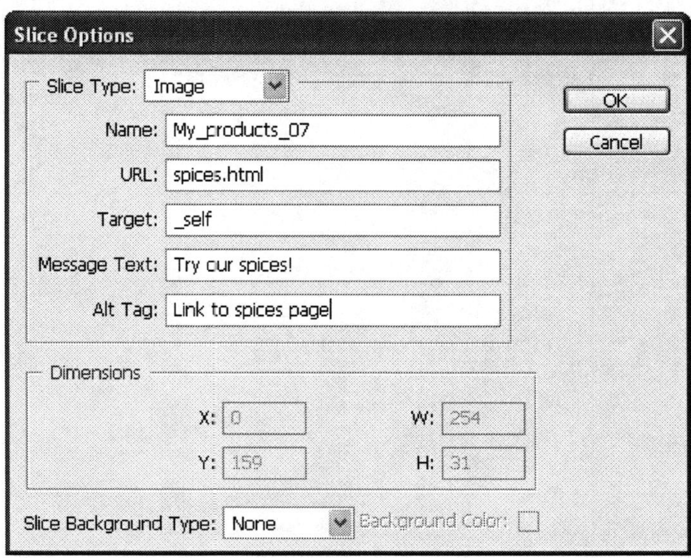

Exhibit 3-1: The Slice Options dialog box

Do it!

A-1:   Assigning links and status-bar messages to slices

Here's how	Here's why
1 Open products	From the current unit folder.
Save the image as **my_products**	
Display slices	(Choose View, Show, Slices.) If necessary.
2 Using the Slice Select tool, right-click **SPICES** on the left	
Choose **Edit Slice Options…**	To open the Slice Options dialog box.
3 In the URL box, enter **spices.html**	This is the file that you want the link to open.
In the Target box, enter **_self**	To have the link open in the original window.
4 In the Message Text box, enter **Try our spices!**	This text will appear in the browser's status bar when the user points to the link.
In the Alt Tag box, enter **Link to Spices page**	
Click **OK**	To close the Slice Options dialog box.
5 Open the Save For Web & Devices dialog box	
6 Preview the image in Internet Explorer	Click the Internet Explorer icon at the bottom of the dialog box.
7 Point to the SPICES slice	
	To observe the tooltip that appears. The link won't work until you save the sliced image and store the generated HTML page in the same location as the document specified by the link.
Observe the browser's status bar	
	It's displaying the text you entered in the Message Text box.
8 Close Internet Explorer	
Click **Cancel**	To close the Save For Web & Devices dialog box.

9	In the image, click **SAUCES**	(Use the Slice Select tool.) To select the Sauces button slice.
	On the options bar, click 	To open the Slice Options dialog box.
10	Assign the URL **sauces.html** with the target **_self**	Enter "sauces.html" in the URL box. Enter "_self" in the Target box.
	Specify the message text **Try our sauces!**	Enter the text in the Message Text box.
	Assign the alternate text **Link to Sauces page**	Enter the text in the Alt Tag box.
	Click **OK**	
11	In the image, click **SEASONINGS**	To select the Seasonings button slice.
	Assign the URL **seasonings.html** with the target **_self**	In the Slice Options dialog box.
	Specify the message text **Try our seasonings!**	
	Assign the alternate text **Link to Seasonings page**	
12	Hide slices	
	Update and close the image	

Topic B: Device Central

This topic covers the following Adobe ACE exam objective for Photoshop CS4.

#	Objective
12.6	Explain how to preview content for a device by using Device Central.

Preview content for mobile devices

Explanation

Increasingly, people are using mobile devices such as cell phones and PDAs (personal digital assistants) to view Web pages and a variety of media. You can use Device Central to create content for mobile devices and to preview how the content will look on specific devices. For example, if you're not sure a particular image will be bright enough when viewed on a cell phone, you can test it in Device Central and then adjust it in Photoshop as necessary.

Create images for mobile devices

You can use Device Central to specify the dimensions, color mode, color profile, and resolution for a specific device and then create a new image with those specifications in Photoshop. To do so:

1 Choose File, Device Central to open Device Central, shown in Exhibit 3-2.

2 Activate the New Document tab.

3 If necessary, in the Online Library list, select the appropriate item and drag it to the Device Sets section.

4 In the list of Device Sets, select the desired device.

5 Click Create to create a Photoshop document that uses the specifications for the selected device.

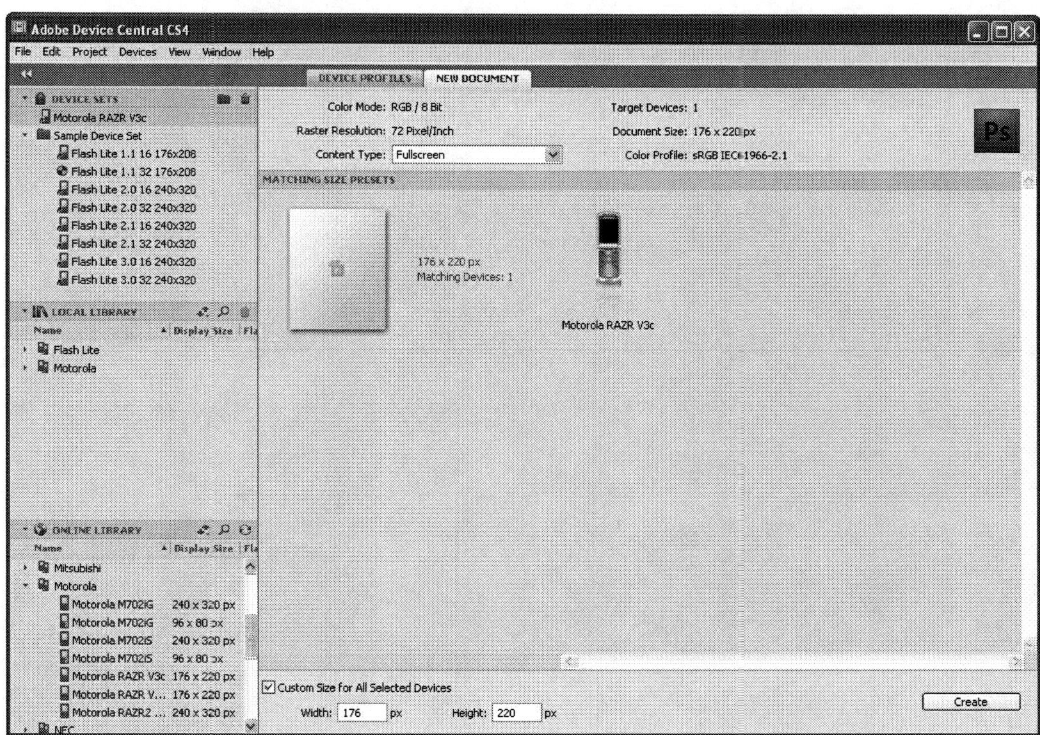

Exhibit 3-2: The New Document tab in the Device Central window

Do it!

B-1:   Creating content for mobile devices

Here's how	Here's why
1 Choose **File,** **Device Central...**	To start Adobe Device Central.
2 Choose **File, New Document In, Photoshop...**	To activate the New Document tab. It shows the settings for the document you'll create.

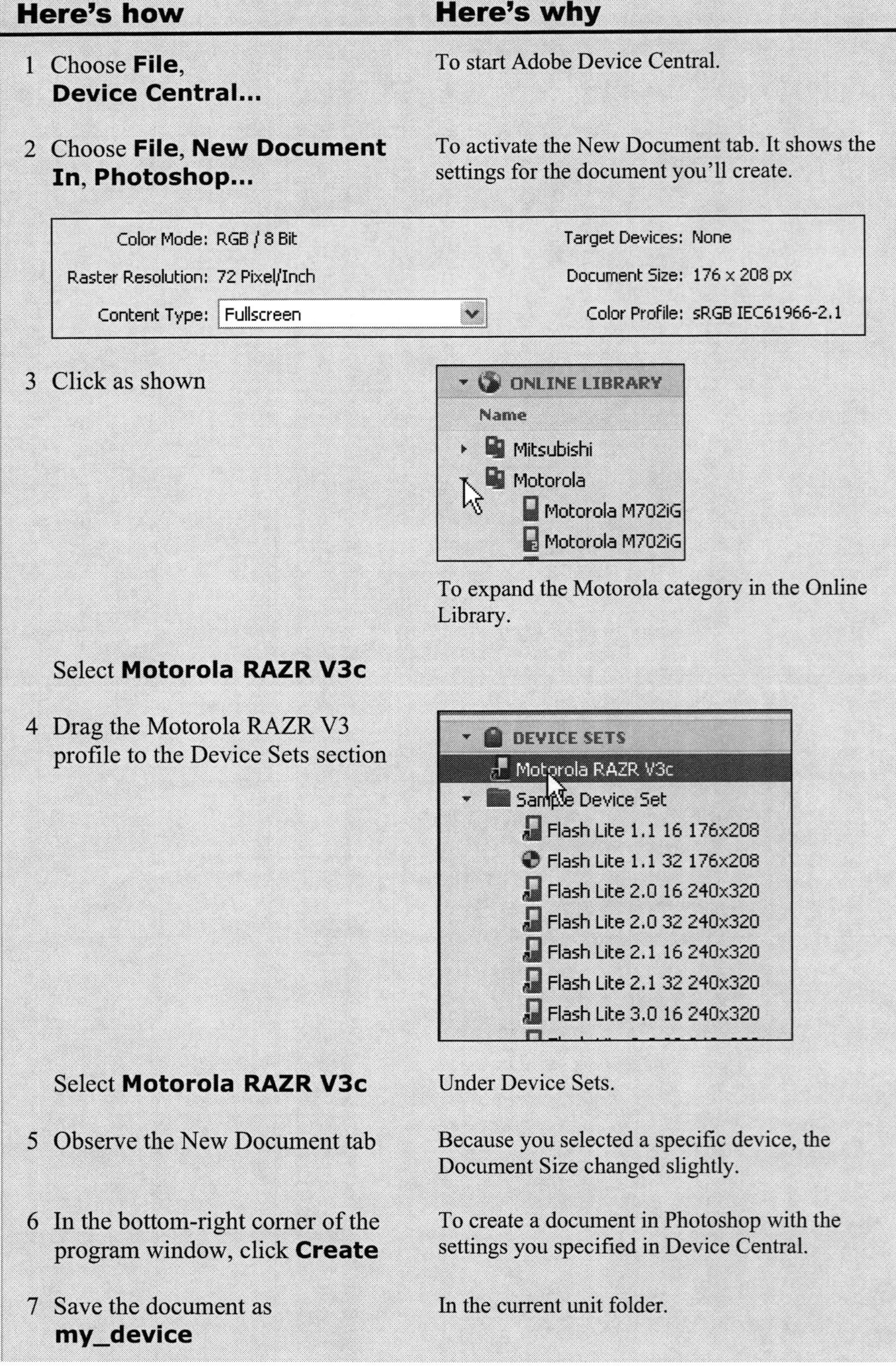

Here's how	Here's why
3 Click as shown	To expand the Motorola category in the Online Library.
Select **Motorola RAZR V3c**	
4 Drag the Motorola RAZR V3 profile to the Device Sets section	
Select **Motorola RAZR V3c**	Under Device Sets.
5 Observe the New Document tab	Because you selected a specific device, the Document Size changed slightly.
6 In the bottom-right corner of the program window, click **Create**	To create a document in Photoshop with the settings you specified in Device Central.
7 Save the document as **my_device**	In the current unit folder.

Optimize images for mobile devices

Explanation

After you create a document in Photoshop by using Device Central, you can add content to it. You can then preview the content in a mockup of the intended device.

To preview and optimize content for a particular mobile device:

1 In Photoshop, choose File, Save for Web & Devices.

2 In the Save For Web & Devices dialog box, click Device Central. The image opens in Device Central, and the Emulator tab shows it on the screen of the device you selected previously, as shown in Exhibit 3-3.

3 Under Display, set the options needed to mimic settings and conditions for the device.

4 If necessary, under Scaling, select an option to fit the image to the device's screen.

5 To adjust the original image, choose File, Return to Photoshop. Then make adjustments in the Save For Web & Devices dialog box, or click Cancel to make other adjustments.

6 Preview the image in Device Central as necessary.

7 To save the image, click Save in the Save For Web & Devices dialog box.

Exhibit 3-3: The Emulator tab in Device Central

Do it!

B-2: Optimizing content for mobile devices

Here's how	Here's why
1 Open Mountaintop sunset	From the current unit folder.
Copy the image	
Close the image	
2 Press CTRL + V	To paste the contents of the Clipboard as a new layer in the My device image.
3 Press CTRL + T	To activate the transform handles.
Resize and position the layer as shown	
Press ↵ ENTER	
4 Open the Save For Web & Devices dialog box	
In the bottom-left corner of the dialog box, click **Device Central**	To open Device Central. The image you've been editing appears on the Emulator tab, within an emulation of the device you selected previously.
5 In the Display panel, check **Timeout**	To preview how the display will look on a device when the screen dims to save battery life. After the specified time (4 seconds, by default), the image dims.
Clear **Timeout**	
6 From the Reflections list, select **Indoor**	To simulate an indoor reflection. The image is mostly still visible.
From the Reflections list, select **Outdoor**	The image looks washed out.

7	Drag the Gamma slider to the left	To darken the midtones in the image.
	Drag the Gamma slider until the sky in the image is more visible	You want to darken the sky in the image so that it's visible when the device is used outdoors, but you don't want to darken it so much that it appears unnaturally dark indoors or when there's no reflection.
8	From the Reflections list, select **Indoor**	To see whether you've overcorrected or whether you need to further reduce the Gamma setting. A setting of about -40% should work for both Indoor and Outdoor settings.
9	Click	To zoom out so that the device emulation appears closer to actual size.
10	Choose **File, Return to Photoshop**	To return to the Save For Web & Devices dialog box.
11	From the Preset list, select **JPEG High**	
	Click **Save**	To open the Save Optimized As dialog box.
	Click **Save**	To save the image.
12	Update and close the image	
	Close Adobe Device Central	Return to Photoshop.

Topic C: Zoomify

Explanation

Typically, photographic images are downsampled before they're displayed on the Web. Downsampling reduces an image's file size to allow faster downloads, and it allows the image to fit in the required space. However, downsampling also removes image detail. If you posted a high-resolution image on the Web so that viewers could see its fine detail, the image would have a large file size, causing it to download slowly. In addition, the image might not fit in a browser window, and viewers would have to scroll to view different parts of it. To resolve these issues, you can use Zoomify to export a high-resolution image for the Web so that viewers can see a smaller version of the entire image that does not require a long download time. Viewers can zoom in on that sample image to see its fine detail, and can pan to view parts of the image in more detail.

Export high-resolution images

When you export an image with Zoomify, you can specify its dimensions so that it fits in a browser window. If you want to show an image in an 800x800-pixel area, you can specify these dimensions to show the entire image. But a user viewing the image will also be able to zoom it and then pan to see different sections, without having to scroll the browser window. The image retains its original dimensions, as shown in Exhibit 3-4. In addition, the image doesn't take any longer to load than would a similar image with the same dimensions.

To export an image by using Zoomify:

1   Choose File, Export, Zoomify to open the Zoomify Export dialog box, shown in Exhibit 3-5.
2   From the Template list, select the desired template.
3   Click Folder to open the Browse for Folder dialog box. Specify a location in which to save the files, and click OK.
4   If desired, edit the Base Name box. This name will appear as part of a URL, so it can't contain spaces or special characters.
5   Under Image Tile Options, specify settings for the main image.
6   Under Browser Options, specify the dimensions of the image area in the browser window.
7   Click OK.

When you export an image with Zoomify, Photoshop creates an HTML file, as well as a folder containing sections of the image at different zoom levels and other files necessary for showing the image in a browser. All of these files (but not the original image) need to be uploaded to a Web server to show the image online. Viewing a Zoomify image in a Web browser requires the Flash Player.

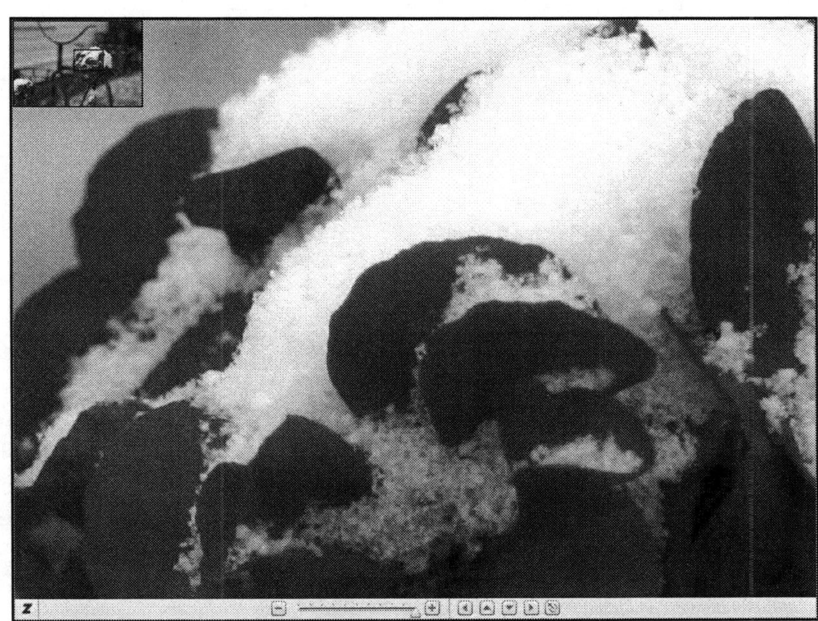

Exhibit 3-4: Viewing a Zoomify image in a browser

Exhibit 3-5: The Zoomify Export dialog box

Do it!

C-1: Exporting an image with Zoomify

Here's how	Here's why
1 Open Snow flower	From the current unit folder.
	You'd like to show this image on the Web at full size.
Save it in Photoshop format as **My snow flower**	In the current unit folder.
2 Choose **File, Save for Web & Devices...**	A warning box appears, stating that this image exceeds the size that Save for Web & Devices was designed for.
Click **Yes**	To close the warning box and open the Save For Web & Devices dialog box.
3 Observe the image's size and download time information	JPEG 1.245M 232 sec @ 56.6 Kbps
	With a slow connection, it would take almost four minutes for this image to load in a Web browser.
Right-click as shown	Size/Download Time (512 Kt Size/Download Time (768 Kt Size/Download Time (1 Mbp Size/Download Time (1.5 Mt Size/Download Time (2 Mbp JPEG 1.245M 232 sec @ 56.6 Kbps
	To display a shortcut menu.
Choose **Size/Download Time (1 Mbps Cable)**	JPEG 1.245M 14 sec @ 1 Mbps
	Even with a high-speed connection, the image would still take a while to load.
4 Click **Cancel**	To close the dialog box. You'll export the image with Zoomify so that it will load more quickly.
5 Choose **File, Export, Zoomify...**	To open the Zoomify Export dialog box.
6 From the Template list, select **Zoomify Viewer with Navigator (Black Background)**	

7	Click **Folder**	To open the Browse for Folder dialog box.
	Navigate to the current unit folder	
	Click **OK**	To specify the output location.
8	Drag the Quality slider all the way to the right	To set the Quality to 12.
9	Edit the Width box to read **800**	
	Edit the Height box to read **600**	The image is wider than it is tall, but you're not sure of the exact ratio. This is an estimate.
10	Verify that Open In Web Browser is checked	
11	Click **OK**	To export the image and open it in Internet Explorer. It appears smaller than its actual size, but you can zoom in to actual size to see various sections of the image.
12	Click anywhere in the image	To activate the Zoomify control.
13	Click in the flower in the center of the image	To zoom in on the section you clicked.
	Click the flower again	To zoom to full size.
14	In the top-left corner of the image, observe the navigator	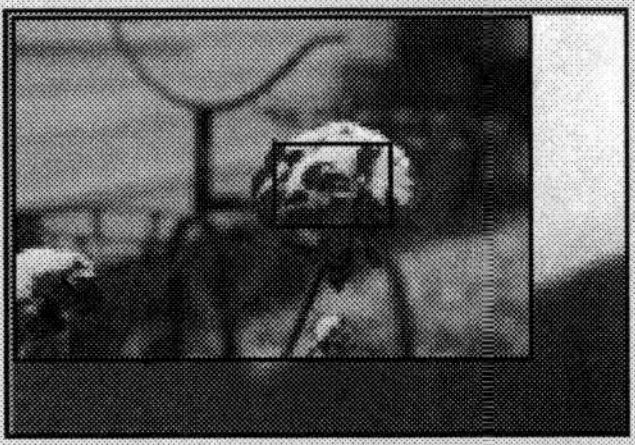 It shows the area of the image you're currently viewing, relative to the whole image.
	Drag within the blue boundary	To change the section of the image displayed.
15	Drag the zoom slider slowly, as shown	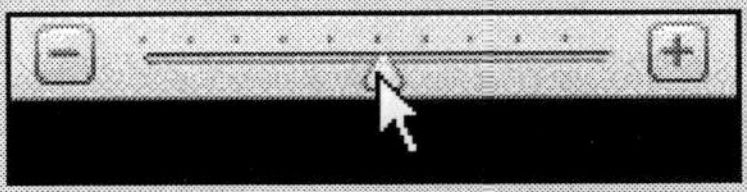 (At the bottom of the image.) To zoom out.
16	Close Internet Explorer	To return to Photoshop.

17 In Windows Explorer, navigate to the current unit folder	Photoshop has created a file named My-snow-flower.html and a folder named My-snow-flower_img.
Open the My-snow-flower_img folder	It contains another folder and two other files: a Shockwave Flash file and an XML file that the browser uses to show the image in the viewer.
Open the TileGroup0 folder	The Zoomify command creates individual images that show sections of the original image at different zoom levels. If you want to show the Zoomify image on a Web page, you'll need to upload both the HTML file and the folder containing these images and the SWF and XML files.
18 Return to Photoshop	
Close the image	

Unit summary: Web and device features

Topic A   In this topic, you used the Slice Options dialog box to specify **URL links** and **alternate text** for individual slices.

Topic B   In this topic, you used **Device Central** to specify the settings for an image that will be displayed on a mobile device. Then you used Device Central to preview the image in a mockup of the device.

Topic C   In this topic, you learned how to use **Zoomify** to export high-definition images that users can pan and zoom on the Web.

Independent practice activity

In this activity, you'll assign links to image slices. You'll also preview an image as it would look in a particular mobile device, and you'll export the image for use in that device. Finally, you'll export an image with Zoomify.

1 Open the navbar image, located in the current unit folder, and save it as **my_navbar**.

2 Assign links to the slices in the nav bar. For example, for the Products tab, the link should be "http://outlanderspices.com/products.html"

3 Update and close the image.

4 Start Device Central.

5 Drag **Nokia N80** from the Online Library list to the Device Sets List. Then select Nokia N80.

6 Create a new document in Photoshop that uses the specifications for this device. Save the file as **My practice device**.

7 Resize and crop the Snow flower image to fit within the dimensions of the new document, as shown in Exhibit 3-6.

8 Preview the image in Device Central. (*Hint*: First, open the Save For Web & Devices dialog box.)

9 Adjust the image's contrast so that it looks reasonably good in both outdoor and indoor conditions.

10 Return to Photoshop, and increase the image's contrast to match the setting you specified in Device Central.

11 Export the image by using the Save For Web & Devices dialog box.

12 Close Device Central.

13 Open the Easter egg image, located in the current unit folder, and save it in Photoshop format as **My Easter egg**.

14 Export the image by using Zoomify. Use a template with a Navigator option, a Width of **450**, and a Height of **300**.

15 Preview the image in a browser, and zoom and pan to see the image detail.

16 Close the browser.

17 Update and close open images.

Exhibit 3-6: The resized and cropped Snow flower image after Step 7 of the independent practice activity

Review questions

1 Where can you specify a link for a slice?

A In the Output Settings dialog box

B In the Save For Web dialog box

C In the Slice Options dialog box

D In the Layers panel

2 When you assign a link to a slice, text that you enter in the Alt Tag box appears __________.

A When you point to the link in a browser

B In the browser's status bar

C In the browser's title bar

D After you click the link

3 True or false? You can export images directly from Device Central.

4 True or false? The settings you apply in Device Central are also applied to the image in Photoshop.

5 By using Zoomify, you can __________.

A Zoom in more closely on an image than you can in Photoshop.

B Create a Web photo gallery with multiple images.

C Export a high-resolution image to a Web browser so that a user can view it at its original size but load it more quickly.

D Export a high-resolution image to a Web browser so that a user can pan and zoom, while reducing the time it takes to load the image.

Unit 4

Automating Web tasks

Unit time: 60 minutes

Complete this unit, and you'll know how to:

A Process multiple images in one step.

B Create droplets that perform actions.

C Create HTML-based Web photo galleries.

D Create multiple variations of a graphic based on variable data.

Topic A: Color and size adjustments

This topic covers the following Adobe ACE exam objectives for Photoshop CS4.

#	Objective
8.4	Given a scenario, describe the best way to process a large number of images through Photoshop.
9.3	Given a scenario, describe the proper color conversion to apply.

Explanation

As you prepare Web images in Photoshop, you should consider how their colors might look in a Web browser. In addition, you might want to use a script to process multiple images at once to optimize them for Web use.

Image preparation

A *color space* is a theoretical representation of color reproduction characteristics that models the gamut of available colors and maps color appearances to values. Photoshop's default working color space is sRGB, which was designed to represent a typical consumer-grade monitor. This setting works well for images created for display on the Web because much of your viewing audience will probably view the image on a monitor with a profile much like sRGB.

When you save an image in Photoshop, the program embeds in the file the color space it was viewed in during editing. Therefore, if another person opens that file, her copy of Photoshop can interpret that color space and display the image as closely as possible to how you saw it. However, Web browsers typically ignore embedded color profiles. Instead, browsers assume that all images use the sRGB color profile. Therefore, an image with an embedded color profile might be displayed differently in a browser than in Photoshop.

When you use the Save For Web & Devices dialog box to optimize and save an image, the default setting is to convert the image to the sRGB color space when it's saved. To deselect this option, choose Convert to sRGB from the Optimize menu.

Browser and platform considerations

You can't control color for Web images as effectively as you can for print images, because Web images will be viewed on many monitors that display colors slightly differently. In addition, the various Web browsers display colors differently. Also, Macintosh computers have a brighter color display than Windows computers.

A very small percentage of the browser audience in the United States uses Macintosh computers, so you should typically use the Windows gamma of 2.2 for Web images. The *gamma* value is the brightness of the midtones in your monitor display. The higher the gamma value, the darker the midtones. Macintosh computers use a gamma of 1.8 by default, but they can be set to a gamma of 2.2. The sRGB color space specifies a gamma of 2.2.

Some older monitors can display only 256 colors (an 8-bit display). On these monitors, a Web image designed to use more than 256 colors might show *browser dithering*, in which several available colors are interspersed among pixels to simulate a color that's not available. This type of dithering is undesirable, but a very small part of the Web audience uses 8-bit monitors, so you might decide not to factor this small audience segment into your design decisions.

Finally, you should consider how long it will take a typical Web browser to download the images on your Web site. Most people today have broadband Internet connections, but sizable percentages still use narrowband. The difference in the time it takes to load most images might be only seconds, but in that time users might decide to browse to a different site, where they can see results more quickly.

The Image Processor script

You can use Photoshop's Image Processor script to process multiple image files in one step. You can convert all images in a specified folder to JPEG, Photoshop (PSD), or TIFF format, and you can specify additional settings.

To use the Image Processor script to process multiple files:

1 In Photoshop, choose File, Scripts, Image Processor to open the Image Processor dialog box, shown in Exhibit 4-1.

2 Under "Select the images to process," specify the images you want to process.

- To process all currently open images, select Use Open Images.
- To specify the folder containing the images you want to process, click the radio button next to Select Folder and then click Select Folder.

3 Under "Select location to save processed images," do one of the following:

- To save the images in a new subfolder within the folder containing the original images, select Save in Same Location.
- To specify a folder in which to save the processed images, click Select Folder.

4 Under File Type, select the file format you want the processed files to use, and specify additional settings for the selected file type. You can check multiple file types to save copies of each image in each file type.

5 Under Preferences, select any actions you want to run on the processed images, specify copyright information for the file metadata, and specify whether you want to embed the color profile in the processed images.

6 Click Run to process the images.

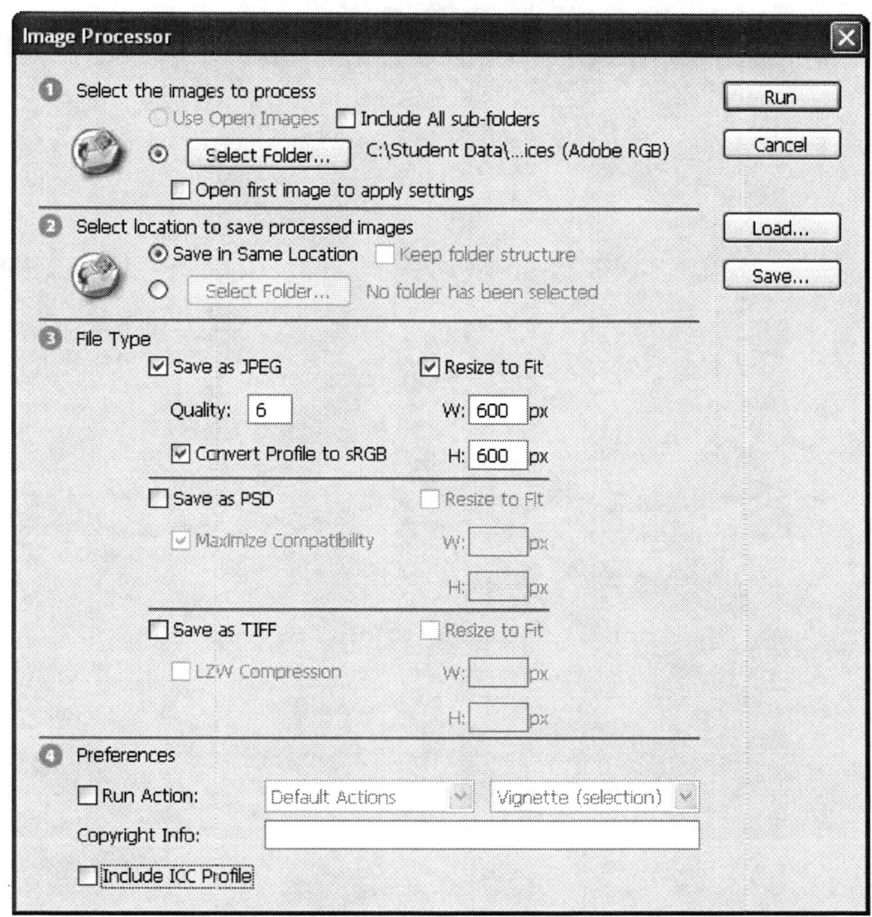

Exhibit 4-1: The Image Processor dialog box

Do it!   ## A-1:   Running the Image Processor script

Here's how	Here's why
1 Choose **File**, **Scripts**, **Image Processor...**	To open the Image Processor dialog box. You'll convert all the images in the Spices (Adobe RGB) folder to JPEG format, and you'll strip out any embedded color profiles.
2 Click **Select Folder**	To open the Choose Folder dialog box.
Select the **Spices (Adobe RGB)** folder	In the current unit folder.
Click **OK**	To return to the Image Processor dialog box.
3 Under "Select location to save processed images," verify that Save in Same Location is selected	To have the Image Processor create a subfolder, inside the selected folder, for storing the processed images.
4 Under File Type, edit the Quality box to read **6**	
Check **Convert Profile to sRGB**	
5 Check **Resize to Fit**	To create images that will be used at a larger size for a Web photo gallery.
In the W and H boxes, enter **600**	
6 Under Preferences, clear **Include ICC Profile**	Because most browsers ignore any embedded color profiles, there is no reason to include it.
Click **Run**	Photoshop processes each image in the folder you selected.
7 In Windows Explorer, open the Spices (Adobe RGB) folder	In the current unit folder.
Open the JPEG folder in a second window	The JPEG folder is in the Spices (Adobe RGB) folder. You'll compare the file sizes of the original images—in the Spices (Adobe RGB) folder—and the new images—in the JPEG folder.
8 In each window, choose **View**, **Details**	
Arrange the windows so that you can see the information in each one	To observe the file sizes of the original and converted images. The file sizes in the JPEG folder are much smaller, and thus more appropriate for Web use.

9 Rename the JPEG folder as
   Spices (Web JPEG)

Move the folder up one level in the hierarchy	So that it's on the same level as Spices (Adobe RGB).

Topic B: Droplets

This topic covers the following Adobe ACE exam objectives for Photoshop CS4.

#	Objective
8.1	Create and use actions.
8.4	Given a scenario, describe the best way to process a large number of images through Photoshop.

Action droplets

Explanation

A *droplet* is a small application generated by Photoshop that you can store on the desktop or in another location on your computer. You can drag image files, or a folder containing files, to a droplet to perform a batch process on the images. You can create droplets from *actions* that perform a defined set of steps on one or more files at a time. Actions can include just about any command you can perform in Photoshop. For example, it's useful to create a droplet for an action that includes multiple steps when you want a more efficient technique for applying those steps to multiple files.

Creating actions

The Actions panel includes some default actions that you can use right away. However, you'll probably need to create your own custom actions to streamline your specific workflows. To create an action, you can use the Actions panel, shown in Exhibit 4-2, to record a set of commands and steps as you perform them.

To create an action:

1 Open an image that's a good example of the type of image you'll apply the action to.

2 Perform any steps that are necessary to prepare this image but that you don't want to record as part of the action.

3 In the Actions panel, click the Create new action button to open the New Action dialog box.

4 Enter a name for the action, and specify a keyboard shortcut for running it.

5 Click Record.

6 Perform the commands and other steps that you want the action to record.

7 In the Actions panel, click the Stop playing/recording button to stop recording action steps.

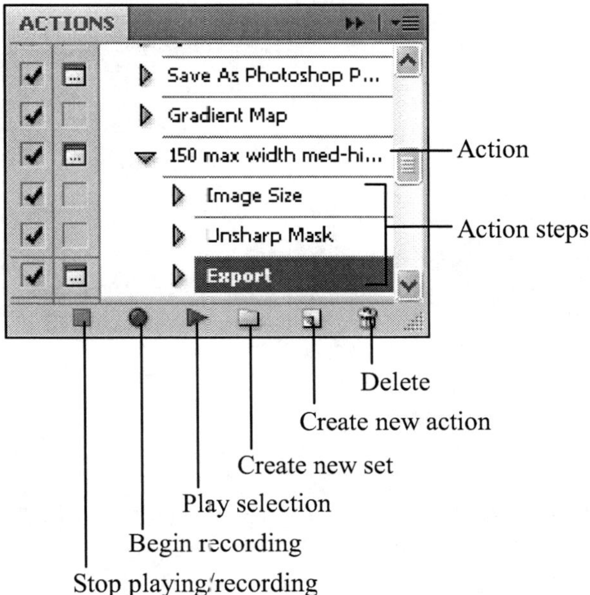

Exhibit 4-2: The Actions panel

Do it!

B-1: Creating an action

Here's how	Here's why
1 Open Cumin 01	In the Granular spices folder, inside the current unit folder.
2 Open the Actions panel	
In the Actions panel, click	(The Create new action button.) To open the New Action dialog box.
Edit the Name box to read **150 max width med-high JPEG**	
Click **Record**	To begin recording the new action.
3 Choose **Image**, **Image Size...**	To open the Image Size dialog box.
Edit the Width box to read **150**	
Click **OK**	The current image is resized, and this step is recorded as part of the action you're creating.
4 Choose **Filter, Sharpen, Unsharp Mask...**	To open the Unsharp Mask dialog box.
Set the Amount value to **90%**	If necessary.
Set the Radius value to **0.8 px**	If necessary.
Click **OK**	
5 Choose **File, Save for Web & Devices...**	To open the Save For Web & Devices dialog box. You'll specify the desired settings, but you won't save the file.
From the Preset list, select **JPEG Medium**	You will change the default Quality setting assigned to the preset you selected.
Set the Quality value to **45**	
6 Press and hold (ALT) and observe the dialog box	To see that pressing Alt changes the Cancel and Done buttons to the Reset and Remember buttons. You want the action you're recording to remember these settings.
Hold (ALT) and click **Remember**	
Release (ALT) and click **Done**	To close the dialog box.

7 In the Actions panel, click 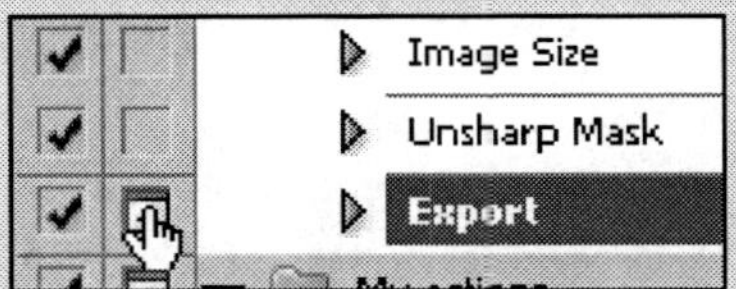	(The Stop playing/recording button.) To stop recording the action.
8 In the Actions panel, click as shown	To toggle the dialog box for the action step. When the action is run, the Save For Web & Devices dialog box will open.
Close the Actions panel	
9 Close the image without updating it	You don't want to apply the settings to this image now.

Creating droplets from actions

Explanation

Creating a droplet is an easy way to apply an action to a file or a folder without having to open Photoshop manually and run the action. Droplets are separate files that you can save on your desktop, for example, or that you can share with other Photoshop users.

To create a droplet from an action:

1 Choose File, Automate, Create Droplet to open the Create Droplet dialog box, shown in Exhibit 4-3.

2 Click Choose to open the Save dialog box. Specify a location in which to save the droplet, and enter a file name. Click Save.

3 From the Set list, select an action set.

4 From the Action list, select the action you want to use for the droplet.

5 Under Play, check the desired options:

- **Override Action "Open" Commands** — Disables any Open commands that might be included in the action you're specifying. Don't check this option if the action contains Open commands for specific files required by the action.

- **Include All Subfolders** — Processes files contained in folders within the folder you specify for the action.

- **Suppress File Open Options Dialogs** —Disables dialog boxes that might otherwise appear when you're opening a file, such as a camera raw image.

- **Suppress Color Profile Warnings** — Turns off color policy messages.

6 From the Destination list, select an option:

- **None** — Leaves the files open after the action is run, unless the action specifies that the files be saved.

- **Save and Close** — Updates the files in their current location after the action is run. Note, however, that selecting this option will cause the original files to be overwritten.

- **Folder** — Opens a dialog box after the action is run so that you can specify a location for saving files.

7 If you selected either Save and Close or Folder from the Destination list, then you can check "Override Action 'Save As' Commands" to disable any Save As commands that might be included in the action you're specifying.

8 If you selected Folder for the destination, then click Choose and specify a folder for the droplet's output. Click OK.

9 Under File Naming, specify the desired options for naming files processed by the droplet.

10 From the Errors list, select an option:

- **Stop For Errors** — Pauses the action until you respond to any error messages.

- **Log Errors To File** — Records any errors during the action without stopping it. If any errors occur, a message will appear after the action is finished.

11 Click OK.

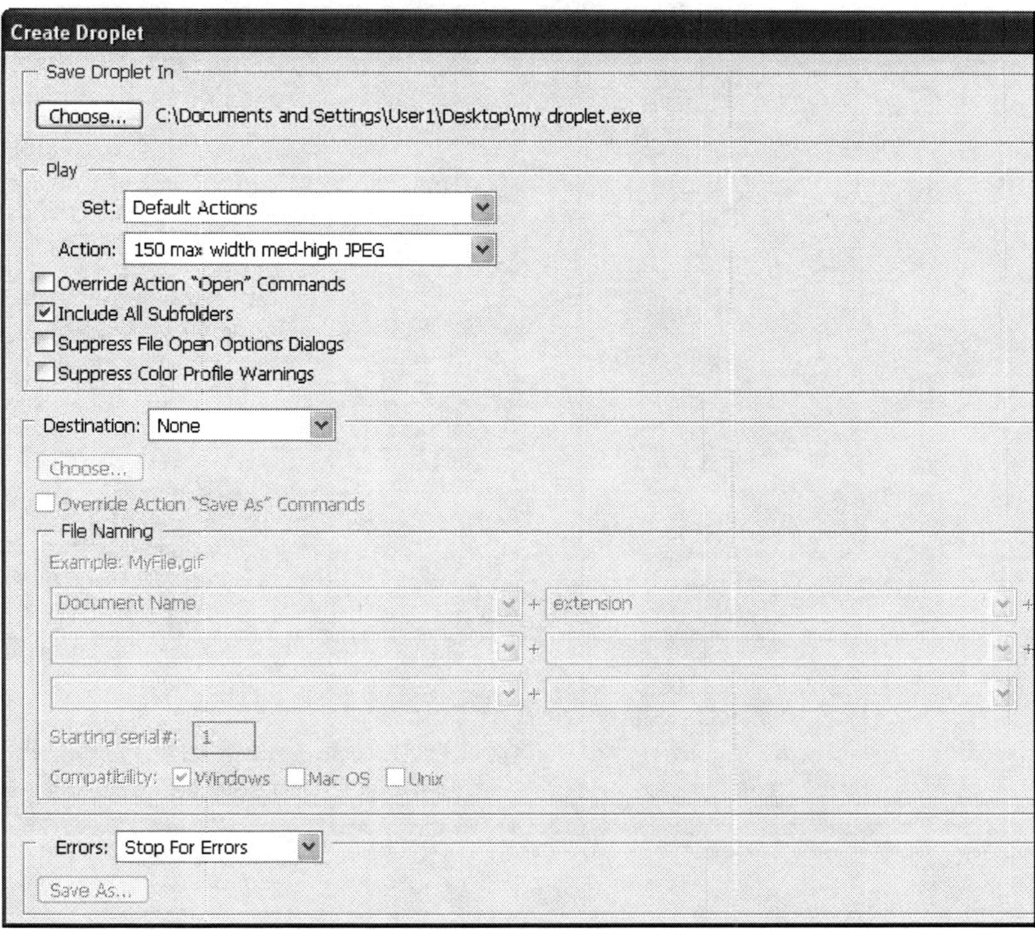

Exhibit 4-3: Options in the Create Droplet dialog box

Do it!

B-2:   Creating a droplet

Here's how	Here's why
1 Choose **File, Automate, Create Droplet...**	To open the Create Droplet dialog box.
2 Click **Choose**	To open the Save dialog box. You'll specify a location for the droplet.
Navigate to the desktop	
Edit the File name box to read **My droplet**	
Click **Save**	To return to the Create Droplet dialog box.

3	From the Action list, select **150 max width med-high JPEG**	(If necessary.) The action you created.
	Check **Include All Subfolders**	You want the action to apply to all images in a folder, even if they're contained in a subdirectory.
		Because the action specifies that the files be saved in a different format, you don't need to specify a separate destination to save them. The original files won't be overwritten.
4	Click **OK**	To save the droplet.
5	Activate Windows Explorer	
	Observe the desktop	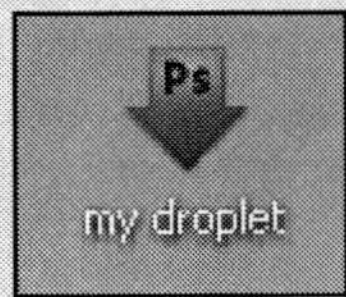 To see that the droplet appears on the desktop.
6	Drag the **Granular spices** folder onto the droplet icon	To begin running the associated action on the files in the folder.
		Each time the action gets to the final step—optimizing the file as a JPEG—the Save For Web & Devices dialog box opens, as you specified.
	Save each file as an image in the Granular spices folder	In the Save Optimized As dialog box, navigate to the Granular spices folder; in the Save as type list, select Images Only (*.jpg); and click Save. Repeat to save each file.
7	Update and close the images	
8	Open the Granular spices folder	(In the current unit folder.) The droplet has created a JPEG-optimized version of each original PNG image.

Topic C: Web photo galleries

This topic covers the following Adobe ACE exam objective for Photoshop CS4.

#	Objective
12.4	Create and upload a complete Web gallery.

Creating HTML-based galleries

Explanation

A *Web photo gallery* is a Web site that has been designed primarily to display images. Both professional and amateur photographers often use Web photo galleries to display their work. A Web photo gallery typically has a page containing image thumbnails that you can click to navigate to pages showing the full-size images.

You can use Adobe Bridge to generate the HTML code necessary to display your images as a Web photo gallery. After generating the files, you can upload them to a Web site. To generate a Web photo gallery:

1   Choose File, Browse in Bridge.
2   In the left side of the Bridge window, navigate to the folder that contains the images you want to use.
3   In the Content section at the bottom of the window, select the images you want to use. If you want to use all of the images in the folder, choose Edit, Select All.
4   If necessary, click the Output tab.
5   In the Output panel, click Web Gallery.
6   From the Template list, select a template.
7   Modify the options in the Site Info and Color Palette sections as desired.
8   Click Preview in Browser. The images and generated HTML files are placed in the folder you specified.
9   In the Create Gallery section of the Output panel, select Save to Disk. Click Browse and select a location. Click Save.

Photoshop CS3 included a Web gallery command in the File menu. You can add the optional Web Gallery plug-in to Photoshop CS4 by installing it from the Goodies folder on the Photoshop CS4 installation disc.

Do it!

C-1: Generating an HTML-based Web photo gallery

Here's how	Here's why
1 Choose **File**, **Browse in Bridge…**	To open Adobe Bridge.
Display the Folders panel	(Choose Windows, Folders Panel.) If necessary.
2 In the Folders panel, navigate to the current unit folder and expand it	On the left side of the window.
Select the **Spices (Web JPEG)** folder	In the current unit folder.
3 Choose **Edit**, **Select All**	To select all of the images in this folder.
Activate the Output panel	If necessary.
In the Output panel, click **WEB GALLERY**	
4 From the Template list, select **Filmstrip**	
In the E-mail Address box, enter **contactus@outlanderspices.com**	
5 In the Color Palette section, click the black color swatch next to Main	(Scroll down.) To open the Color dialog box.
Select a medium gray color	
Click **OK**	
6 Click **Preview in Browser**	To preview the Web gallery.
Click one of the thumbnail images	To view a larger image.
Close the browser window	To return to Bridge.
7 Scroll to the bottom of the Output panel	To view the Create Gallery section.
Select **Save To Disk**	
Click **Browse**	

8	Navigate to the Web Gallery folder in the current unit folder	You'll save the Web gallery files here.
	Click **OK**	
	Click **Save**	The Create Gallery dialog box appears.
	Click **OK**	To close the dialog box.
9	Close Adobe Bridge	To return to Photoshop.
10	In Windows Explorer, navigate to the **Web Gallery\Adobe Web Gallery\resources\images** folder in the current unit folder	
		To view the folders within the images folder. Images were saved in large, medium, and thumbnail formats.

Topic D: Data-driven graphics

This topic covers the following Adobe ACE exam objective for Photoshop CS4.

#	Objective
8.6	Create variables.

Creating multiple versions of an image

Explanation

Many projects require you to generate multiple versions of an image with slightly different data in each. For example, you might want to generate several versions of a Web banner ad, with each one highlighting a different product. To do this, you can create a template graphic with placeholder data, and then have Photoshop generate each variation based on data you provide.

Variables

You can create data-driven graphics with three types of variable elements:

- **Text replacement** — Replaces text in a type layer with text specific to each graphic you generate.
- **Visibility** — Shows or hides the contents of a layer. Use this variable type for text that might or might not apply to each graphic you generate. For example, use it for text such as "On sale now!" (because not all items will always be on sale).
- **Pixel replacement** — Replaces the pixels in a layer with pixels from another source file. Use this variable type for things such as product photos that should be different in each version of the graphic.

Exhibit 4-4 shows an example of each type of variable data used to generate three versions of a banner advertisement.

Exhibit 4-4: Three versions of a data-driven graphic

The original image used to generate the data contains only placeholders denoting where the actual data should appear, as shown in Exhibit 4-5.

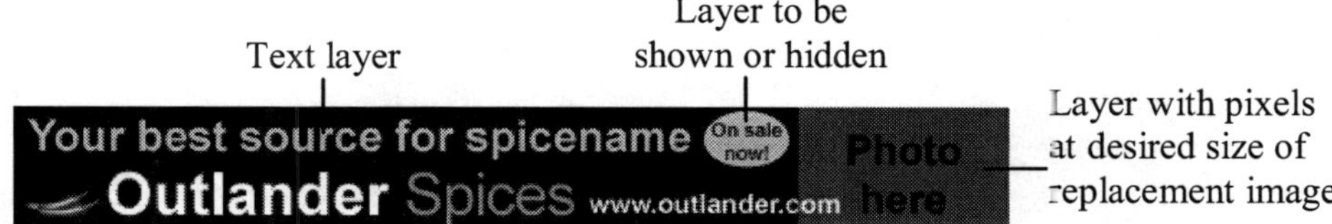

Exhibit 4-5: A template file with placeholder data

Creating data-driven graphics

To create a data-driven graphic:

1 Create a template graphic with placeholders, such as the one shown in Exhibit 4-5.

2 If you plan to create a pixel-replacement variable, then create a separate image file for each version of the graphic you want to generate. The image files do not have to match the size at which they will appear in the template; the process of merging them can resize them automatically. (In Exhibit 4-4, the pictures of cinnamon, nutmeg, and bay leaf are all separate image files that are much larger than the banner ad.)

3 Choose Image, Variables, Define to open the Variables dialog box, shown in Exhibit 4-6. Assign a variable name to each layer you want to change in the exported versions. The variable name must begin with a letter, underscore, or colon and cannot contain spaces or special characters. (If you're familiar with creating databases, each variable you create is similar to a field in a database table.)

4 Click Next to display the Data Sets panel of the Variables dialog box. In this panel, you define a data set for each version of the graphic you want to output. In each data set, you assign a value to each variable you created, as shown in Exhibit 4-7. (If you're familiar with creating databases, each data set is similar to a record in a database table.)

For pixel replacement, you can choose how the substituted image should be sized. In most cases, the Fit method works well because it resizes the image to fit the space while retaining the original image's proportions.

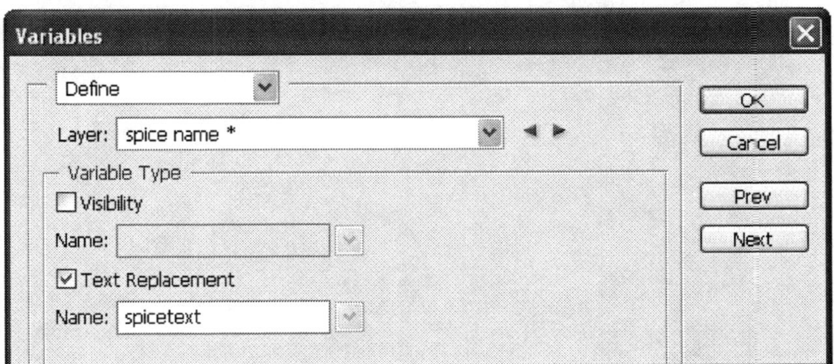

Exhibit 4-6: Assigning a variable to a layer

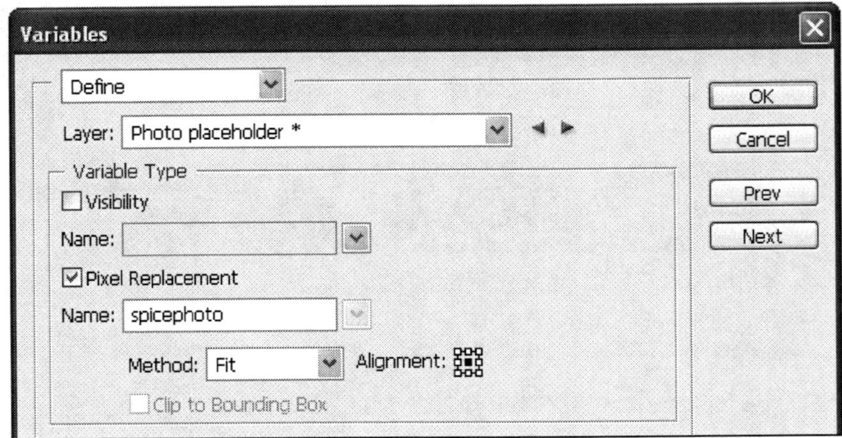

Exhibit 4-7: Assigning values to variables in one data set

You might want to create a table to organize your planning and data for the graphic, as shown below. If you create many data sets, it might not be practical to create a column for each one, but a few should suffice for planning purposes.

Layer	Variable	Type	cinnamon data-set values	nutmeg data-set values	bayleaf data-set values
spice name	spicetext	Text replacement	cinnamon!	nutmeg!	bay leaf!
Photo placeholder	Spicephoto	Pixel replacement	Cinnamon.png	Nutmeg.png	Bay leaf.png
On sale now	Salevis	Visibility	Visible	Not visible	Visible

Do it!   ## D-1:   Creating variables for a data-driven graphic

Here's how	Here's why
1 Open banner	In the Banner ad variables folder in the current unit folder.
Save the file as **outlanderbanner**	The base name you use will be included in each version of the graphic you generate.
2 Choose **Image**, **Variables**, **Define...**	To open the Variables dialog box. You'll assign variables to three layers so their contents or visibility can change in each generated version.
3 From the Layer list, select **spice name**	(If necessary.) You'll replace the text in this layer with the actual name of the spice for each generated version.
Under Variable Type, check **Text Replacement**	To indicate that the text on this layer will be replaced by data from the data set for each generated version of the graphic.
Edit the Name box to read **spicetext**	To specify the variable name, which must be one word with no spaces.
4 Click ▶	(To the right of the Layer list.) To select the next layer, which is named "On sale now."
Under Variable Type, check **Visibility**	To indicate that this layer might or might not be shown in each generated version of the graphic.
Edit the Name box to read **salevis**	To specify the variable name.
5 Click ▶	To select the next layer, which is named "Photo placeholder."
Check **Pixel Replacement**	To indicate that the pixels on this layer will be replaced with those from another image for each generated version of the graphic.
Edit the Name box to read **spicephoto**	The variable name.
In the Method list, verify that Fit is selected	To have the replacement images be sized to fit proportionally in the space of the original Photo placeholder layer.

Data sets

Explanation

After you've assigned variables to layers, you must create a separate data set for each version of the graphic you want to output. For small amounts of data, you can enter the data in the Data Sets section of the Variables dialog box, as shown in Exhibit 4-8. When you need to create a large number of variations, you might want to import data from a text file by clicking Import in the Variables dialog box.

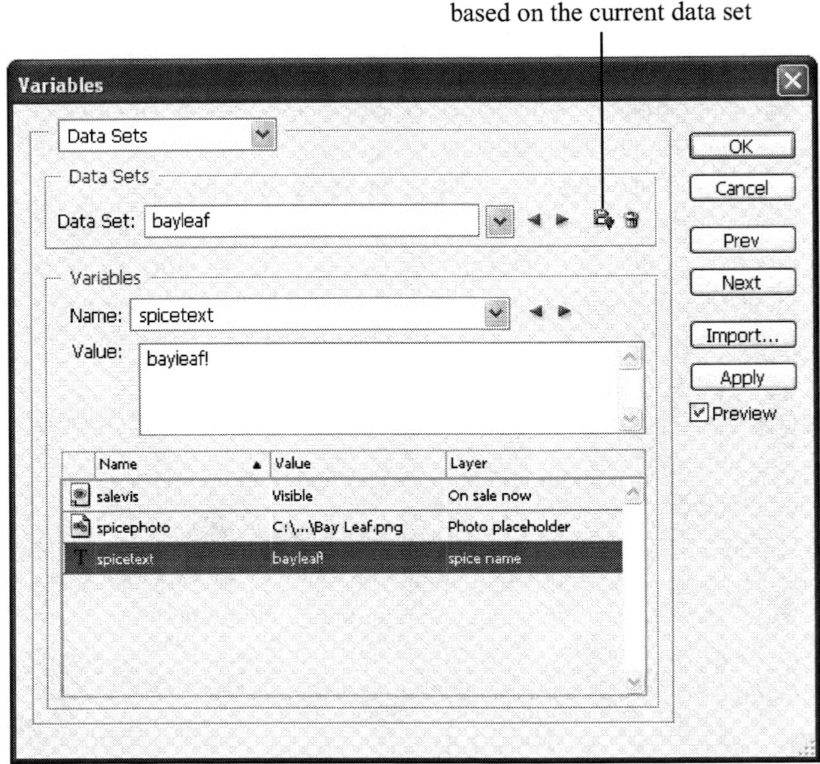

Exhibit 4-8: Specifying settings for a data set

Do it!   **D-2:   Creating data sets**

Here's how	Here's why
1 In the Variables dialog box, click **Next**	To view Data Sets information.
2 Click 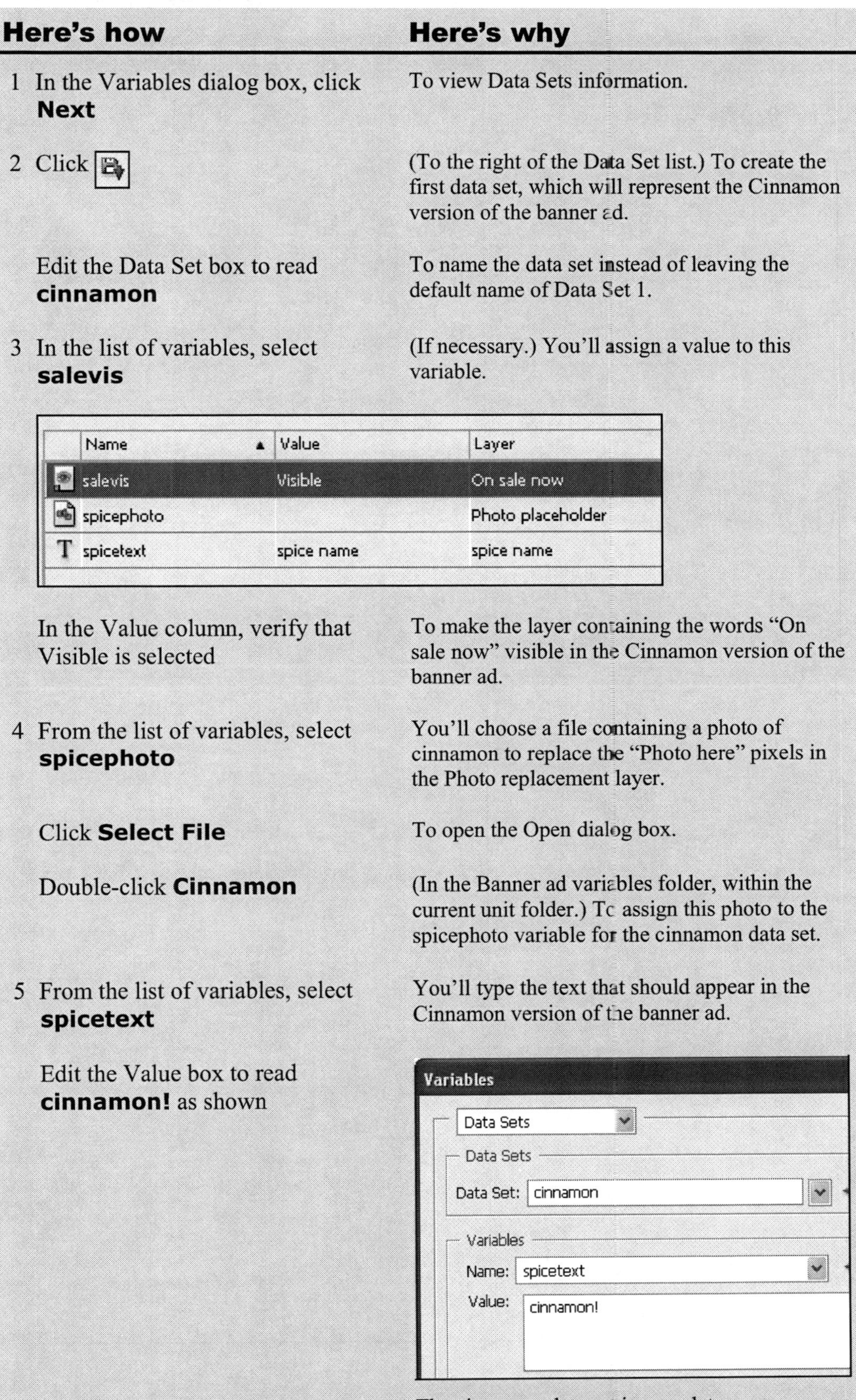	(To the right of the Data Set list.) To create the first data set, which will represent the Cinnamon version of the banner ad.
Edit the Data Set box to read **cinnamon**	To name the data set instead of leaving the default name of Data Set 1.
3 In the list of variables, select **salevis**	(If necessary.) You'll assign a value to this variable.

Name	▲	Value	Layer
salevis		Visible	On sale now
spicephoto			Photo placeholder
T spicetext		spice name	spice name

In the Value column, verify that Visible is selected	To make the layer containing the words "On sale now" visible in the Cinnamon version of the banner ad.
4 From the list of variables, select **spicephoto**	You'll choose a file containing a photo of cinnamon to replace the "Photo here" pixels in the Photo replacement layer.
Click **Select File**	To open the Open dialog box.
Double-click **Cinnamon**	(In the Banner ad variables folder, within the current unit folder.) To assign this photo to the spicephoto variable for the cinnamon data set.
5 From the list of variables, select **spicetext**	You'll type the text that should appear in the Cinnamon version of the banner ad.
Edit the Value box to read **cinnamon!** as shown	

The cinnamon data set is complete.

6 Check **Preview**

To see the data applied to the image.

Move the Variables dialog box so you can see the image file

(If necessary.) The word "cinnamon," the cinnamon picture, and the "On sale now!" layer are displayed in this version of the banner ad.

7 Create a data set for the nutmeg version of the image, with the following values:

(Click the "Create a new data set based on the current data set" button, and enter the values indicated.) To create a second version of the banner ad.

Data-set name: **nutmeg**
salevis value: **invisible**
spicephoto value: **Nutmeg**
spicetext value: **nutmeg!**

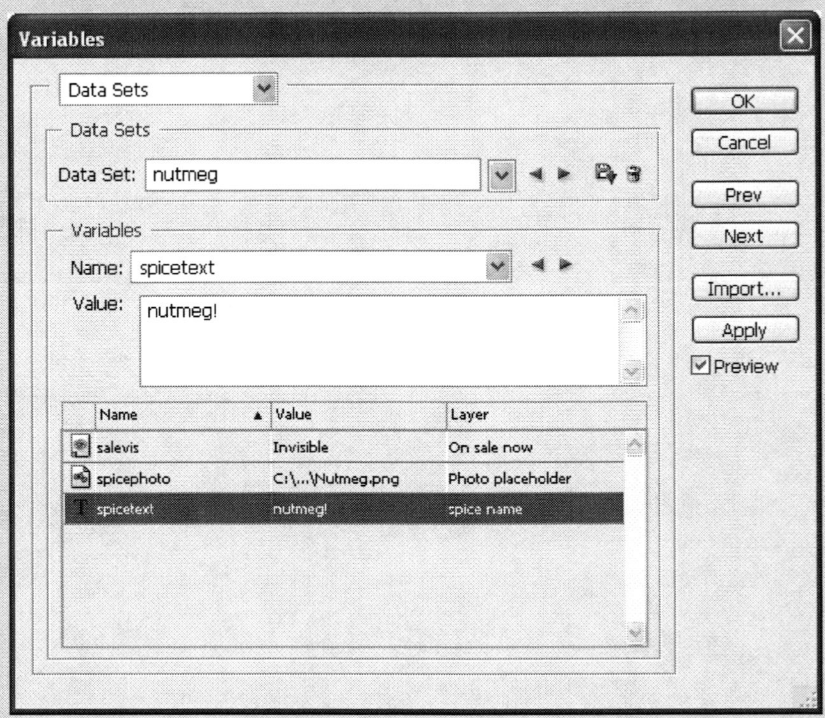

8 Create a data set for the bayleaf version of the image, with the following values:

   Data-set name: **bayleaf**
   salevis value: **visible**
   spicephoto value: **Bay leaf**
   spicetext value: **bay leaf!**

To create a third version of the banner ad.

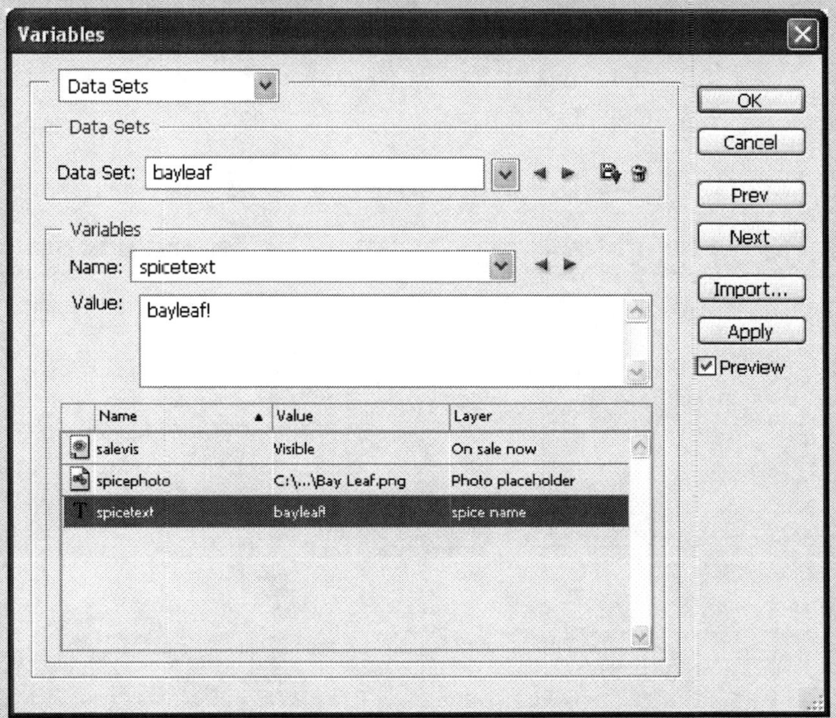

9 Click ▶ a few times to cycle through the data sets, observing the changes in the image window

(Click the arrow under Data Sets.) To check that you entered the data as intended.

10 Click **OK**

To close the Variables dialog box.

Exporting data-driven graphics

Explanation

After you've created the variables and data sets for your data-driven graphic, you're ready to export a separate image file for each data set. From Photoshop, you can generate only Photoshop-format files.

To export data-driven graphics:

1   Choose File, Export, Data Sets as Files to open the Export Data Sets as Files dialog box.
2   Click Select Folder to open the Browse For Folder dialog box. Specify a location for saving the files, and click OK.
3   If desired, under File Naming, set options for naming the exported files.
4   Click OK.

Do it!

D-3:   Exporting a separate file for each data set

Here's how	Here's why
1 Choose **File, Export, Data Sets as Files...**	To open the Export Data Sets as Files dialog box.
2 Click **Select Folder**	To designate the folder in which the new images should be created.
Navigate to and select the **Banner ad variables** folder	If necessary.
Click **OK**	
3 Click **OK**	To export the images with the default naming convention (the base name plus the data-set name).
4 Open outlanderbanner_bayleaf, outlanderbanner_cinnamon, and outlanderbanner_nutmeg	(From the Banner ad variables folder.) To verify that each file appears as intended.
5 Update and close all files	

Unit summary: Automating Web tasks

Topic A   In this topic, you used the **Image Processor script** to process multiple images in one step.

Topic B   In this topic, you used the Actions panel to generate an **action**. You also created a **droplet** based on the action so you could apply the action to multiple files at once.

Topic C   In this topic, you used Adobe Bridge to create **Web photo galleries** that use HTML to display your images.

Topic D   In this topic, you used the Variables dialog box to specify variables and data sets in order to create a **data-driven graphic**. You then exported multiple variations of that graphic.

Independent practice activity

In this activity, you'll use the Image Processor script on a folder of images. You'll also create an action, generate a droplet that runs the action, and apply the droplet to a folder. Then you'll generate a Web photo gallery.

1 Use the Image Processor script on the **Prepared foods (Adobe RGB)** folder, located in the Practice folder in the current unit folder. Save the images in JPEG format in the same folder.

2 Create an action that saves images as **JPEG** with a Quality setting of **20**, and name the action **Medium-low JPEG**. (*Hint*: Use the Save For Web & Devices dialog box, and turn on the dialog box in the action.)

3 Create a droplet named **My practice droplet** that uses the Medium-low JPEG action.

4 Apply the droplet to the **Food on dishes** folder, which is located in the Practice folder in the current unit folder.

5 Generate a Web photo gallery from the "Practice\Prepared foods (Adobe RGB)\JPEG" folder, located in the current unit folder. (*Hint*: The "Practice\Prepared foods (Adobe RGB)\JPEG" folder was generated as part of Step 1 in the independent practice activity. Create a Web Gallery folder within the Practice folder.) Preview the Web Gallery.

6 Close Internet Explorer and Adobe Bridge.

7 Update and close any images.

Review questions

1 What script can you run to automatically specify the size, JPEG quality, and sRGB color space for images?

2 True or false? A large percentage of Web viewers' monitors can display only 256 colors.

3 You've created a custom action that applies specific settings to an image, and you want to share the action with colleagues. To save the action as a separate file, what do you need to create?

  A A script.

  B A batch.

  C A droplet.

  D You can't save actions as separate files

4 How can you process a large number of images through Photoshop?

  A Use Adobe Bridge to group the files.

  B Use the Image Processor script.

  C Create macros.

  D Use the Save for Web & Devices dialog box on each file.

5 Photoshop can generate a Web photo gallery in which of the following formats? [Choose all that apply.]

  A HTML

  B Flash

  C QuickTime

  D PDF

6 To generate a Web photo gallery, what should you use?

  A The Save For Web dialog box

  B The File, Automate, Web Photo Gallery command

  C The Actions panel

  D The File, Save dialog box

7 What types of variable elements can be used in data-driven graphics? [Choose all that apply.]

  A Layer styles

  B Text replacement

  C Pixel replacement

  D Layer visibility

8 How can you specify variables to generate multiple versions of an image?

  A Specify each variable as an alpha channel.

  B Specify each variable as a layer style.

  C Choose Image, Variables, Define.

  D Create an action to define each variable.

Unit 5

Animation

Unit time: 50 minutes

Complete this unit, and you'll know how to:

A Use the Animation and Layers panels to create animations.

B Use Photoshop to output animations for use on the Web.

Topic A: Creating animation

This topic covers the following Adobe ACE exam objectives for Photoshop CS4.

#	Objective
1.4	Given a scenario, describe the best way to resize an image.
12.3	Explain how to create an animated Web image.

Animated images

Explanation   You can use Photoshop to create animations, which are a series of frames in which each frame can display different content. Changing the content slightly from frame to frame creates the appearance of motion as the animation plays. You can export animations from Photoshop to the GIF format.

Simple animation

You use the Animation panel to create animation frames, and you use the Layers panel to specify the content that will be visible in each frame. To create a simple animation:

1   Open the image you'll use as the basis for the animation.

2   Choose Window, Animation to open the Animation panel, shown in Exhibit 5-1. The Animation panel contains a single frame, which displays the content of the image you opened.

3   In the Animation panel, click the "Duplicates selected frames" button to create a new frame that contains content matching that of the previous frame.

4   To change the content of a frame, select it and then use the Layers panel to make your changes. You can use any of the following techniques:

- Turn visibility on or off for individual layers.

- Change the position of layer content so it appears to move from one frame to the next.

- Change the opacity of individual layers over a series of frames to make the content fade in or out.

- Change the blending mode for individual layers.

- Add or modify layer styles for individual layers.

5   To specify how long each frame is displayed before the animation advances to the next frame, first select one or more frames. Then, from the Delay pop-up menu below one of the selected frames, choose the frame delay time you want to use.

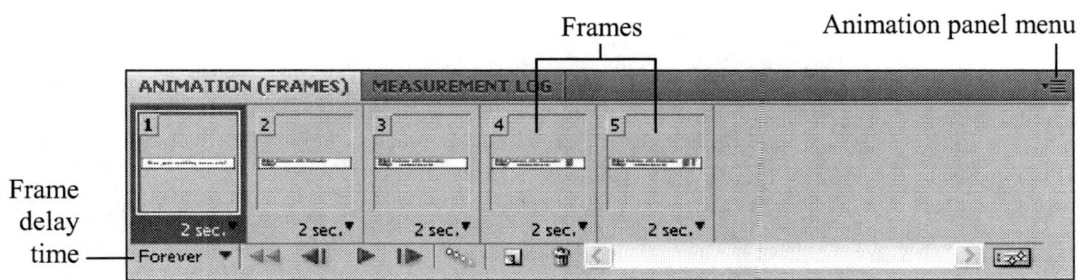

Exhibit 5-1: The Animation panel

To play the animation, select the first frame in the Animation panel and click the Play button. When the animation is playing, the Play button is replaced by the Stop button, which you can click to stop the animation. The Animation panel's controls are shown in Exhibit 5-2.

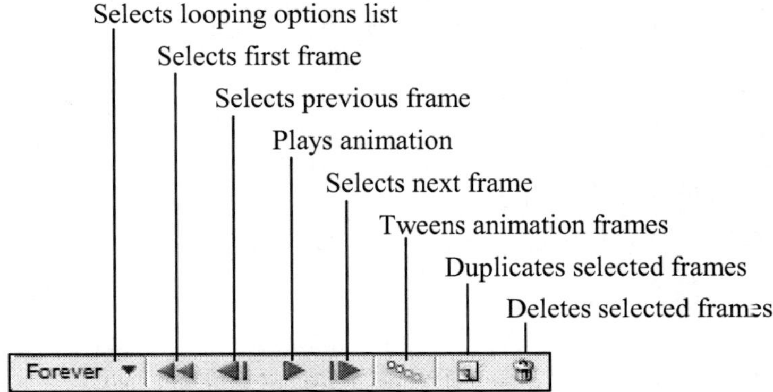

Exhibit 5-2: Animation panel controls

Do it!

A-1: Creating animation frames

Here's how	Here's why
1 Open videobanner	From the current unit folder.
Save the image as **my_videobanner**	
2 Choose **Window, Animation**	To display the Animation panel.
In the Animation panel, click [⬛]	(The "Duplicates selected frames" button.) To duplicate the first frame.
3 In the Layers panel, hide the top two type layers	To hide those layers in the second frame.
Show the **Order Cooking with Outlander today!** type layer	**Order *Cooking with Outlander today!***
4 In the Animation panel, click [⬛]	To duplicate frame 2.
Show the **Available on DVD or VHS** type layer	
5 Duplicate the third frame	Click the "Duplicates selected frames" button.
Show the DVD layer	
6 Duplicate the fourth frame	
Show the VHS layer	
7 In the Animation panel, select frame 1	You will select all of the frames.
Press (SHIFT) and select frame 5	

8 Under frame 1, from the Delay
   pop-up menu, choose **2.0**

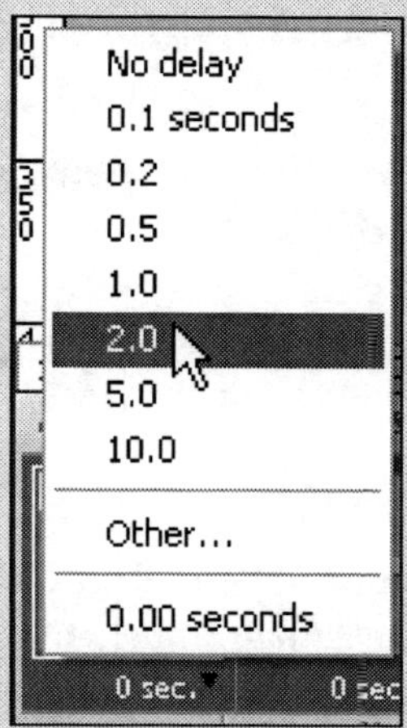

(Click the frame delay time to display the pop-up menu.) To set a two-second delay between the selected frames.

 9 Select frame 1

10 In the Animation panel, click   (The Plays animation button.) To observe the animation.

   Click   (The Stops animation button.) To stop the animation.

11 Update the image

Tweening animation frames

Explanation

Tweening automatically adds or modifies frames between two specified frames. This creates smoother animation, with each frame displaying a slightly different version of the content. You can quickly create the multiple frames you'll need by creating only the first and last frames for a given effect and then using the Tweening dialog box to add the frames in between. The additional frames will display progressively varying layer attributes (position, opacity, or layer effects) between the starting and ending frames.

For example, if you want to animate a word moving across the screen, create one frame with the word in its starting position and a second frame with the word in its ending position. Then select the two frames and use the Tween dialog box to specify how many intermediate frames to create. The frames you add will display the word at intermediate positions between the starting and ending positions. The more intermediate frames you add, the smoother the animation will play, but the larger the resulting file size will be.

To tween a pair of animation frames:

1   Create two frames: one with the starting content, and one with the ending content.

2   Select the two frames and click the "Tweens animation frames" button to open the Tween dialog box, shown in Exhibit 5-3.

3   Enter the settings you want to use, and click OK.

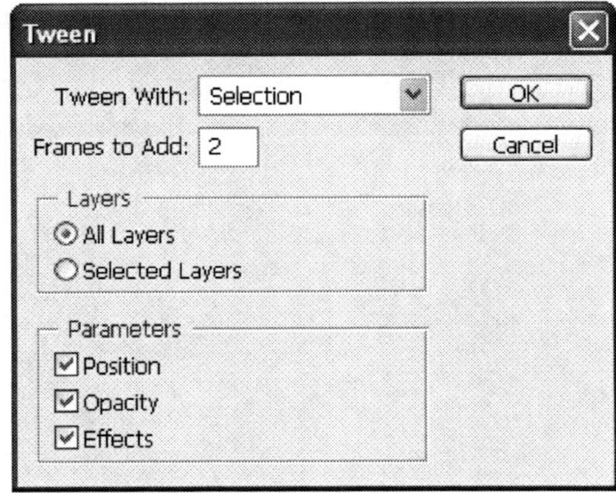

Exhibit 5-3: The Tween dialog box

The Tween dialog box includes the options described in the following table:

Option	Description
Tween With	Select the frames to tween with. When you're tweening two selected frames, the only available option is to tween based on those frames. If you select a single frame before opening the Tween dialog box, you can tween the selected frame with either the previous or the next frame.
Frames to Add	Specify the number of intermediate frames to add.
Layers	Choose All Layers (to vary all layers in the selected frames) or Selected Layers (to vary only the selected layer in the selected frames).
Parameters	Check any or all of the parameters to adjust them for the layers in the intermediate frames.

Do it!   **A-2: Tweening**

Here's how	**Here's why**
1 Select frame 1	If necessary.
Duplicate the frame twice	Click the "Duplicates selected frames" button twice.
Select frame 1, and hide the zip! layer	The change is applied to frame 1, but not to frames 2 and 3.
2 Select frame 2	
Select the **zip!** layer	
3 Select the Move tool	
Point in the image; then press (SHIFT) and drag to the right so that only the letter "z" shows	**some z** Pressing Shift constrains the movement of the layer horizontally.
4 Select frame 3	The word "zip!" is in the final position. You'll use the Tween button to add two frames between frames 2 and 3, with "zip!" showing at intermediate positions between its original and final positions.
5 Select frames 2 and 3	
In the Animation panel, click [▱]	(The "Tweens animation frames" button.) To open the Tween dialog box.
Edit the Frames to Add box to read **2**	
Click **OK**	To create the additional frames.
6 Select frame 2	(If necessary.) To view the word "zip!" in its original position, with only the "z" showing.
Select frame 3	To view the first tweened frame, which positions "zip!" farther to the left.
Select frame 4	To view the second tweened frame, with "zip!" even farther to the left.

7	Select frames 2–4	
	From the Delay pop-up menu for any of the selected frames, choose **No delay**	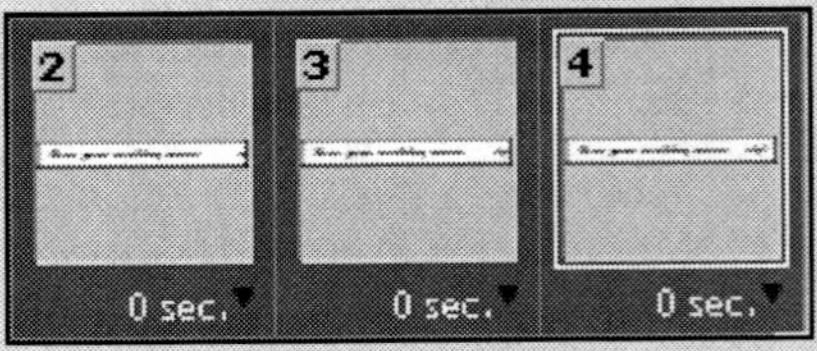 To specify a delay of zero seconds for each of the selected frames.
8	Click 	To move to the first frame.
	Play the animation	After two seconds, the word “zip!” moves into the image from the right.
	Stop the animation	
9	Update the image	

Creating an animated motion blur

Explanation

Another way to simulate motion is to apply a motion blur to the moving object in some of the frames in an animation. You can use a motion blur to give the impression of very fast motion without having it look too jumpy.

You can use the Free Transform command to skew content to add to the perception that it is moving. To do this, choose Edit, Free Transform. Press Ctrl and drag one of the handles to skew the content.

To apply a motion blur to an animation in Photoshop:

1   In the Animation panel, select the frame in which you want to display a motion blur.

2   In the Layers panel, select the layer that contains the content you want to blur.

3   If you want the original, unblurred layer content to appear before or after the motion-blurred animation, then you'll need to duplicate the layer first. Changing the pixel content of a layer affects that layer in all frames, so you'll need a blurred version and an unblurred version that you can show and hide as necessary throughout the animation.

4   If you want the blurred content to look as if it's leaning forward or backward as it races across the screen, then use the Edit, Free Transform command to skew the layer content. Press Ctrl and drag a transform handle to skew the layer content.

5   Choose Filter, Blur, Motion Blur to open the Motion Blur dialog box.

6   In the Angle box, specify the angle at which the blurred object should appear to be moving.

7   In the Distance box, specify the blur's intensity (from 1 to 999). A higher Distance value moves the blurring over a greater distance, giving the impression that the object is moving faster.

8   Click OK.

9   Duplicate or tween the blurred frame as necessary to finish the effect.

Do it!

A-3: Blurring to simulate fast motion

Here's how	Here's why
1 In the History panel, select the last Duplicate Frame history state	To back up to the state before you added the "zip!" animation. You'll create an animation that looks smoother than the two-frame tween you created earlier. You'll start with three identical frames at the beginning of the animation.
2 In the Animation panel, select frame 1	
Hide the zip! layer	
3 Select frame 2	You will duplicate the zip! layer to make a blurry copy, but you'll retain the sharp version as well because you don't want a blurry version in all frames.
From the Animation panel menu, choose **New Layers Visible in All Frames**	To clear this option.
4 In the Layers panel, duplicate the zip! layer	(Drag the zip! layer to the "Create a new layer" button.) The duplicate layer appears above the original layer in the stacking order.
Hide the zip! layer	
Rename the duplicate layer **zip! blur**	
Select the **zip! blur** layer	If necessary.
5 Choose **Edit, Free Transform**	
While pressing CTRL + SHIFT, drag the top-middle transform handle to the left, as shown	me zip!
	To skew the word "zip!" Pressing Ctrl skews the layer, while pressing Shift constrains the transformation horizontally.
Press ↵ ENTER	To complete the transformation.

6   Choose **Filter**, **Blur**, **Motion Blur...**

To open the Motion Blur dialog box. An alert box appears, warning that the type layer will be rasterized, making the text no longer editable as text.

Click **OK**

To close the alert box.

Edit the Distance box to read **25**

Click **OK**

7   Duplicate frame 2

8   In the original frame 2, drag the blurred **zip!** to the indicated position

In frame 3, drag the blurred **zip!** to the indicated position

You will not create a tween this time because you want the movement to look really fast, and even one extra frame would look too slow (and add unnecessarily to the file size).

In frame 4, show the **zip!** layer

(If necessary.) Not the zip! blur layer.

9   Select frames 2 and 3

Set the delay time to **No delay**

10   Play the animation, starting with frame 1

Stop the animation

11   Update the image

Topic B: Animation output options

Explanation

After creating an animation in Photoshop, you can save it in a format that supports animation. Photoshop can optimize the animation for the GIF format, which supports animation and can be viewed in a browser without requiring a plug-in. If you're using Photoshop Extended, you can also export the animation as a QuickTime movie, in several formats.

Optimizing animations for the GIF format

You can use Photoshop's Save for Web & Devices command to export a copy of the animation as an *Animated GIF* file. You can optimize the animation just as you'd optimize a static GIF image. In addition, the Save For Web & Devices dialog box includes buttons for navigating among the animation frames and playing the animation, as shown in Exhibit 5-4.

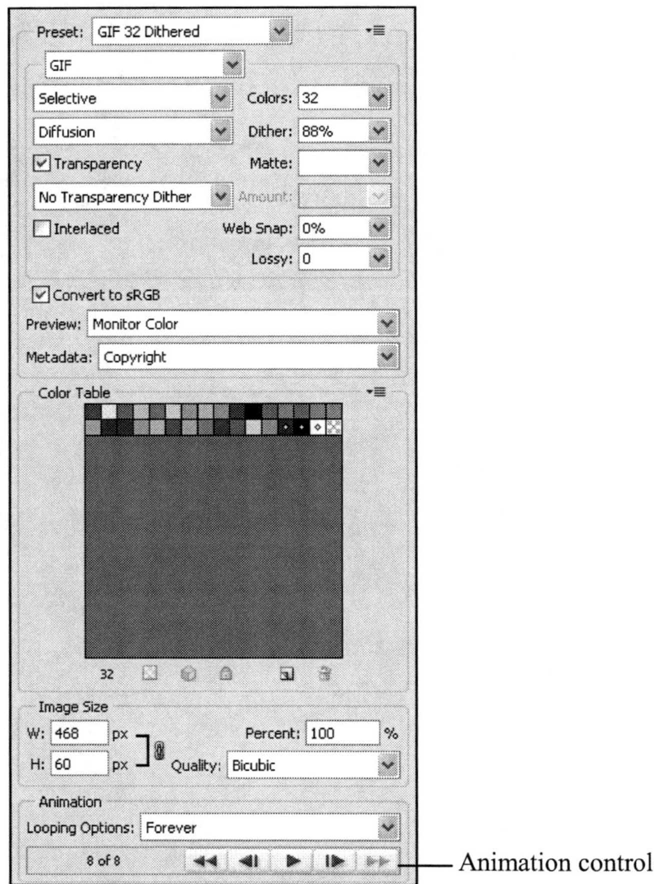

Exhibit 5-4: The Save For Web & Devices dialog box options for an animated GIF

Do it!

B-1: Saving an animation in Animated GIF format

Here's how	Here's why
1 Choose **File, Save for Web & Devices...**	To open the Save For Web & Devices dialog box.
2 From the Preset list, select **GIF 32 Dithered**	(If necessary.) You'll preview the animation in the Save For Web & Devices dialog box.
In the Looping Options list, verify that Forever is selected	(Below the Color Table.) To make the animation loop continuously.
Click ▶	The Plays animation button, near the bottom-right corner of the dialog box.
3 Click **Save**	To open the Save Optimized As dialog box.
4 From the Save as type list, select **HTML and Images (*.html)**	To save both the image and an HTML file for a Web page that includes the animation.
Navigate to the current unit folder	
Click **Save**	
5 In Internet Explorer, open my_videobanner	In the current unit folder.
Observe the animation	The animation loops by default.
6 Close Internet Explorer	To return to Photoshop.
Update and close the image	

Unit summary: Animation

Topic A

In this topic, you used the Animation and Layers panels to create simple **animations**. You also learned how to **tween** animation frames to create smoother motion effects. Finally, you created a **motion blur** to simulate fast movement.

Topic B

In this topic, you used Photoshop's Save For Web & Devices command to save an animation in the **GIF** format.

Independent practice activity

In this activity, you'll create an animation. You'll then export it in the GIF format, and you'll preview the animation in Internet Explorer.

1 Open bookbanner and save the image as **my_bookbanner.psd**.

2 Create an animation that begins with the zip! layer hidden.

3 Create a second frame, with a blurred version of the zip! layer positioned almost completely off the top-right corner of the image, as shown in Exhibit 5-5. Leave only a small portion of the letter "z" showing. (*Hint*: In the second frame, duplicate the zip! layer and show the duplicated layer. Use a filter to blur the layer.)

4 Create a third frame, with the zip blurred layer positioned just to the right and a little below the word "some," as shown in Exhibit 5-6.

5 Create a fourth frame that displays the original zip! layer and hides the zip blurred layer as shown in Exhibit 5-7. The word "zip!" should not be in the same location as the blurred version of the word in the third frame.

6 Set delays for the frames as follows:
   frames 1 and 4: 2 seconds;
   frames 2 and 3: 0.2 seconds.

7 Export the animation in Animated GIF format.

8 Update and close the image.

9 Preview the animation in Internet Explorer by opening the HTML file generated by Photoshop.

10 Close Internet Explorer.

11 Close Photoshop.

Exhibit 5-5: The second frame after Step 3 is completed

Exhibit 5-6: The third frame after Step 4 is completed

Give your cooking some zip!

Exhibit 5-7: The fourth frame after Step 5 is completed

Review questions

1 True or false? All frames in an animation must have the same duration.

2 Creating additional frames by automatically blending two existing ones is called __________.

3 To simulate fast motion without creating several additional frames, you can __________ a layer's contents.

4 In which file format can you create animation in Photoshop?

  A GIF

  B JPEG

  C TIFF

  D PNG

5 True or false? You can export an animated GIF by using the Save For Web & Devices dialog box.

6 How can you change the appearance of a single animation frame without affecting other animation frames?

  A In the Animation panel, select a frame; then choose Specify Frame Visibility from the panel menu.

  B In the Animation panel, select a frame; then choose a filter from the Filter menu.

  C In the Animation panel, select a frame; then use the Channels panel to specify the channels that are visible.

  D In the Animation panel, select a frame; then use the Layers panel to specify the layer content that is visible.

Appendix A
ACE exam objectives map

This appendix covers these additional topics:

A ACE exam objectives for Photoshop CS4 with references to corresponding coverage in ILT Series courseware. .

Topic A: Comprehensive exam objectives

Explanation

The following table lists the Adobe Certified Expert (ACE) exam objectives for Photoshop CS4 and indicates where each objective is covered in conceptual explanations, hands-on activities, or both.

#	Objective	Course level	Conceptual information	Supporting activities
1.1	Describe how to arrange panels and save workspaces. (Includes: arranging and docking panels, customizing menus and shortcuts, and saving workspaces.)	Basic	Unit 1, Topic B	B-2
		Advanced	Unit 5, Topic D	D-1, D-2
1.2	Describe how to use tabbed documents and the application frame. (Includes: window management (not panel/workspace management), includes screen modes, canvas rotation, n-up views.)	Basic	Unit 1, Topic B	B-1
		Web	Unit 1, Topic B	B-1
1.3	Describe options for changing the document view and zoom level. (Includes: GPU-assisted pan and zoom techniques.)	Basic	Unit 1, Topic B	B-3
1.4	Given a scenario, describe the best way to resize an image. (Includes: canvas Size dialog box, Image Size dialog box, resampling options, Free Transform, Options bar, resolution concepts.)	Basic	Unit 6, Topic A Unit 6, Topic B	A-1, A-2 B-2
		Advanced	Unit 4, Topic C	C-2
		Web	Unit 5, Topic A	A-3
1.5	Add metadata to an image in Adobe Photoshop	Basic	Unit 7, Topic B	B-2
1.6	Explain the advantages of and when you would use 32-bit, 16-bit, and 8-bit images.	Basic	Unit 4, Topic A	A-1
		Print	Unit 2, Topic A Unit 2, Topic D	A-1
1.7	Explain the advantages of different file format choices when saving a Photoshop document. (Includes: file formats, compression methods, color support.)	Basic	Unit 7, Topic A Unit 7, Topic B	A-1 B-5
		Print	Unit 5, Topic B	B-2
2.1	Explain how to correct tonal range and color in Photoshop by using the Adjustments panel. (Includes: setting black point and white point, using Curves/Levels, Hue/Saturation vs. Vibrance, Auto Color, new Curves interface, Selective Color, new color correction UI)	Basic	Unit 4, Topic B Unit 4, Topic C	B-1, B-2, B-3 C-1, C-2, C-3
		Print	Unit 3, Topic B Unit 3, Topic C Unit 3, Topic D Unit 3, Topic F Unit 4, Topic C Unit 5, Topic A	B-2 C-1, C-2 D-1, 2, 3 F-1 C-1 A-1

#	Objective	Course level	Conceptual information	Supporting activities
2.2	Given a painting tool, adjust options appropriately and paint on a layer. (Includes: Brush tool, Pencil tool, blending modes, Options bar.)	Basic Advanced	Unit 5, Topic B Unit 4, Topic A	B-3 A-2
2.3	Create, edit, and save a custom brush.	Advanced	Unit 4, Topic A	A-3
2.4	Given a scenario, explain which retouching tool would be most effective. (Includes: Healing, Spot healing, Patch tools and options, Clone Source panel.)	Basic	Unit 5, Topic A	A-2, A-3, A-4, A-5
2.5	Create and use gradients and patterns.	Advanced	Unit 1, Topic B Unit 1, Topic C	B-1, B-2, B-3 C-1
2.6	Explain how to use filters and the Filter Gallery.	Basic Web Print	Unit 5, Topic D Unit 1, Topic A Unit 2, Topic A Unit 2, Topic B Unit 2, Topic C	D-1 A-2 A-3 B-1 C-1, C-2, C-3
3.1	Given a scenario, create a selection using the appropriate tool. (Includes: Quick Selection, Lasso tools, Magic Wand, Marquee tool, Color Range, luminosity shortcut.)	Basic Advanced	Unit 2, Topic A Unit 2, Topic B Unit 2, Topic B	A-1 – A-9 B-1, B-2
3.2	Save and load selections.	Basic	Unit 2, Topic A	A-3
3.3	Move and transform selections.	Basic	Unit 2, Topic B	B-3
3.4	Modify and preview a selection using Refine Edge.	Basic	Unit 2, Topic B	B-4
4.1	Create and arrange layers and layer groups.	Basic Advanced	Unit 3, Topic A Unit 3, Topic B Unit 1, Topic A Unit 4, Topic C	A-1, A-2, A-3 B-1, B-2 A-3 C-1
4.2	Given a scenario, select, align, and distribute multiple layers in an image.	Basic	Unit 3, Topic A Unit 3, Topic B	A-3 B-1
4.3	Explain the uses of layer comps, and compare to layer groups.	Advanced	Unit 4, Topic C Unit 4, Topic F	C-1 F-1
4.4	Given a scenario, explain the use of layer Blending Options.	Basic	Unit 3, Topic D	D-2
4.5	Create and edit layer effects.	Basic	Unit 3, Topic D	D-3
4.6	Create and edit layer styles.	Basic	Unit 3, Topic D	D-3
4.7	Explain how to convert an image to black and white with the most control.	Print	Unit 5, Topic A	A-1, A-2

#	Objective	Course level	Conceptual information	Supporting activities
5.1	Explain the uses of masks and channels.	Advanced	Unit 2, Topic A Unit 2, Topic B Unit 2, Topic C Unit 2, Topic D	A-1, A-2 B-1, B-2 C-1, C-2 D-1
5.2	Given a scenario, use the Masks panel and painting tools to create and edit a layer mask.	Advanced	Unit 2, Topic B Unit 2, Topic C	B-1, B-2 C-1, C-2
5.3	Create, view, and edit channels.	Advanced	Unit 2, Topic A	A-2
		Print	Unit 3, Topic D	D-2
5.4	Explain the difference between a layer mask and a vector mask.	Advanced	Unit 3, Topic C	C-1
5.5	Explain why you would use a clipping mask.	Advanced	Unit 2, Topic D Unit 3, Topic C	D-1 C-2
5.6	Convert to or from a selection, a channel, a layer mask, a vector mask, and a Quick Mask.	Advanced	Unit 2, Topic A Unit 2, Topic B	A-2 B-1
6.1	Create shape layers and paths using the Pen and Shape tools.	Advanced	Unit 3, Topic A Unit 3, Topic B Unit 3, Topic C Unit 3, Topic D	A-1 – A-4 B-1, B-2, B-3, C-1 D-1
6.2	Explain the advantages of using vector drawing tools versus pixel-based tools.	Advanced	Unit 3, Topic A	A-1
6.3	Given a scenario, manage paths using the Paths panel.	Advanced	Unit 3, Topic A	A-2, A-3, A-4
6.4	Given a scenario, alter the properties of type.	Basic	Unit 3, Topic C	C-1, C-2, C-3
		Advanced	Unit 3, Topic D Unit 4, Topic B	D-1 – D-4 B-1
7.1	Describe the advantages of using Adobe Camera Raw to process digital camera raw files.	Print	Unit 2, Topic A	A-1
7.2	Given a Camera Raw adjustment setting, explain the purpose of that setting.	Print	Unit 2, Topic A	A-1
7.3	Export files from Camera Raw.	Print	Unit 2, Topic A	A-1
7.4	Given a scenario, import files directly from a camera using Bridge. (Includes: Adobe Photo Downloader options.)	Basic	Unit 7, Topic D	D-1
7.5	Given a scenario, describe the best way to apply one image's adjustments to many others. (Includes: Synchronize in Camera Raw, or copy and paste settings in Bridge)	Print	Unit 2, Topic A	A-1, A-2

#	Objective	Course level	Conceptual information	Supporting activities
7.6	Apply keywords and metadata to images by using Bridge. (Includes: Keywords panel, Metadata panel, and metadata templates)	Basic	Unit 7, Topic B	B-3, B-4
7.7	Given a scenario, find a specific group of files out of a large collection in Bridge.	Basic	Unit 7, Topic B	B-2
8.1	Create and use actions.	Advanced	Unit 5, Topic A Unit 5, Topic B	A-2 – A-5 B-1, B-2
		Web	Unit 4, Topic B	B-1, B-2
8.2	Create and use a batch action.	Advanced	Unit 5, Topic C	C-1
8.3	List and describe the automation features in Photoshop.	Advanced	Unit 5, Topic A	A-1
		Print	Unit 2, Topic D	D-1
8.4	Given a scenario, describe the best way to process a large number of images through Photoshop.	Advanced	Unit 6, Topic C	C-1
		Web	Unit 4, Topic A Unit 4, Topic B	A-1 B-1, B-2
8.5	Describe the difference between actions and scripting.	Advanced	Unit 5, Topic A	A-1
8.6	Create variables.	Web	Unit 4, Topic D	D-1, D-2, D-3
9.1	Describe the process and components of Photoshop color management. (Includes: profiles, working spaces, rendering intents, settings.)	Print	Unit 1, Topic A Unit 1, Topic B Unit 1, Topic C Unit 1, Topic D	A-2 B-2 C-1 D-2
9.2	Configure the Color Settings dialog box.	Print	Unit 1, Topic C Unit 4, Topic A	C-1 A-2, A-3, A-4
9.3	Given a scenario, describe the proper color conversion to apply. (Scenarios include: To CMYK for prepress, to a different color space for Web or video.)	Basic	Unit 4, Topic A	A-1, A-2
		Print	Unit 1, Topic A Unit 1, Topic C Unit 4, Topic A	A-2 A-1, A-2
		Web	Unit 4, Topic A	A-1
9.4	Given a scenario about a color management problem, describe the proper action to take.	Print	Unit 1, Topic A Unit 1, Topic B Unit 1, Topic C Unit 1, Topic D Unit 3, Topic A	 B-2 C-1
9.5	Discuss the relationship between color gamut and rendering intents.	Print	Unit 1, Topic A Unit 1, Topic D	A-1 D-2
9.6	Explain the purpose and use of the Proof Setup command.	Print	Unit 1, Topic D Unit 4, Topic A	D-1 A-2

#	Objective	Course level	Conceptual information	Supporting activities
10.1	Given a scenario, create and edit a Smart Object. (Scenarios include: create from Camera Raw files, imported vector objects, and layers.)	Advanced / Print	Unit 4, Topic C / Unit 2, Topic A	C-2, C-3, C-4 / A-1
10.2	Create and edit Smart Filters.	Advanced	Unit 4, Topic E	E-1, E-2
10.3	Given a scenario, use Vanishing Point to edit in perspective.	Advanced	Unit 4, Topic D	D-1
10.4	Explain how to use features that handle images moving to and from video workflows. (Includes: Pixel aspect ratio, document presets, Video Preview.)	Advanced	Unit 4, Topic G	G-1, G-2
10.5	Create, edit, and convert an HDR image.	Print	Unit 2, Topic D	D-2, D-3
10.6	Describe how to use Photomerge to create a panorama.	Print	Unit 2, Topic D	D-1
11.1	Given a scenario, describe how to set up the Print dialog box.	Basic / Print	Unit 7, Topic C / Unit 1, Topic D	C-1 / D-2
11.2	Using the Print dialog, position an image at a given size and location on a sheet of paper.	Basic	Unit 7, Topic C	C-1
11.3	Configure the Print dialog for color-managed output to a high-quality inkjet printer. (Includes: set the correct Color Management options, understand the relationship of Photoshop to the printer driver.)	Print	Unit 1, Topic D	D-2
11.4	Given a scenario, prepare an image for use in a printed Adobe InDesign document. (Includes: flattened CMYK, layered RGB with layer comps, Photoshop PDF with vector layers.)	Print	Unit 4, Topic A	A-1
11.5	Set up the Print dialog box to proof one device on another.	Print	Unit 1, Topic D	D-3
12.1	Given a scenario, choose the appropriate Save for Web options for a Web graphic. (Includes: file format, transparency, and metadata inclusion.)	Basic / Web	Unit 7, Topic A / Unit 1, Topic A / Unit 1, Topic B / Unit 1, Topic C / Unit 1, Topic D / Unit 2, Topic D	A-1 / A-1, A-2, A-3 / B-1, B-2 / C-1, C-2 / D-1, D-2, D-3 / D-2

#	Objective	Course level	Conceptual information	Supporting activities
12.2	Explain the options in the Save for Web and Devices dialog box.	Basic	Unit 7, Topic A	
		Web	Unit 1, Topic A Unit 1, Topic B Unit 1, Topic C Unit 1, Topic D Unit 2, Topic D	A-1, A-2, A-3 B-1, B-2, C-1, C-2 D-1, D-2, D-3 D-2
12.3	Explain how to create an animated Web image.	Web	Unit 5, Topic A Unit 5, Topic B	A-1, A-2, A-3, B-1
12.4	Create and upload a complete Web gallery.	Web	Unit 4, Topic C	C-1
12.5	Explain how to create a sliced Web image.	Web	Unit 2, Topic A Unit 2, Topic B Unit 2, Topic C Unit 2, Topic D Unit 3, Topic A	 B-1 – B-4 C-1 D-1, D-2 A-1
12.6	Explain how to preview content for a device using Device Central.	Web	Unit 3, Topic B	B-1, B-2

Course summary

This summary contains information to help you bring the course to a successful conclusion. Using this information, you will be able to:

A Use the summary text to reinforce what you've learned in class.

B Determine the next courses in this series (if any), as well as any other resources that might help you continue to learn about Adobe Photoshop CS4.

Topic A: Course summary

Use the following summary text to reinforce what you've learned in class.

Unit summaries

Unit 1

In this unit, you learned about factors that influence **image file size**, and you used the Image Size command to **downsample** images for Web use. You also used the **Trim** command to remove excess pixels from image borders. Then you used the Save for Web & Devices command to **optimize** an image in the JPEG and GIF formats for Web use, and you specified optimization settings to achieve a **target file size**. Next, you applied a **lossiness** setting to specified areas of an image, while masking other areas. Finally, you learned about formats that support **transparency**, and about Web browsers that support partial transparency. You also learned how to select **matte colors** for GIF and JPEG images to smoothly blend opaque pixels with transparency or with a Web page's background color.

Unit 2

In this unit, you created a **Web-page layout** by using a customized grid and Smart Guides. Next, you learned how to create **user slices** and **layer-based slices**. In addition, you used the Slice Select tool to move and resize slices. You also optimized individual slices and **linked slices**. Then you set slices to display **HTML text** instead of image data. Finally, you customized slice names and **exported** a sliced image as a set of image files with an associated HTML document.

Unit 3

In this unit, you used the Slice Options dialog box to specify **URL links** and **alternate text** for individual slices. Then you used **Device Central** to specify the settings for an image intended for use on a mobile device, and you used Device Central to preview the image in a mockup of the device. Finally, you learned how to use **Zoomify** to export high-definition images that users can pan and zoom on the Web.

Unit 4

In this unit, you used the **Image Processor script** to process multiple images in one step. Then you used the Actions palette to generate an **action**, and you created a **droplet** based on the action. You also created **Web photo galleries** that use HTML to display your images. Finally, you used the Variables dialog box to specify variables and data sets in order to create a **data-driven graphic**, and you exported multiple variations of that graphic.

Unit 5

In this unit, you created simple **animations**. You also learned how to **tween** animation frames to create smoother motion effects, and you created a **motion blur** to simulate fast movement. You then used Photoshop's Save For Web & Devices command to save an animation in the **GIF** format.

Topic B: Continued learning after class

It is impossible to learn to use any software effectively in a single day. To get the most out of this class, you should begin working with Adobe Photoshop CS4 to perform real tasks as soon as possible. We also offer resources for continued learning.

Next courses in this series

This is the last course in this series.

Other resources

For more information, visit www.axzopress.com.

Photoshop CS4: Web Design

Quick reference

Button	Shortcut keys	Function
	Z	Increases image magnification.
	ALT + Zoom tool	Switches the Zoom tool to the Zoom Out tool.
	H	Pans an image within a window.
	X	Switches the current foreground and background colors.
	K	Creates slices in an image.
	O	Selects slices.
	CTRL + '	Shows or hides the grid.
	Q	In the Save For Web & Devices dialog box, turns slice visibility on and off.
		In the Save For Web & Devices dialog box, launches Internet Explorer.

Glossary

Action

A saved series of steps that Photoshop performs in sequence and that you activate with a single click in the Actions palette.

Animated GIF

A GIF file that contains multiple frames that are displayed in sequence so that the image changes over time.

Badge

An icon that appears on a slice to identify the slice's type or to provide other information about the slice.

Broadband connection

A high-speed connection faster than 56 kbps (kilobits per second).

Browser dithering

A browser's method of simulating a color that the monitor can't display; the browser does this by alternating a pattern of colors that the monitor can display. Browser dithering is typically noticeable only with monitors set to display 256 colors.

Color management

A process that adjusts colors as necessary to achieve a close match when an image is displayed or printed on different devices.

Color space

A theoretical representation of color reproduction characteristics that models the gamut of available colors and maps color appearances to values. You can think of a color space as a variant within a color mode.

Compression

Reducing a file's size by simplifying the data in the file.

Dithering

Simulating a color by alternating a pattern of two or more other colors. For example, a dithered pattern of yellow and blue pixels can appear green.

Downsampling

Reducing the number of pixels in an image without changing its basic appearance.

Droplet

A small application that Photoshop generates to perform a batch process. You typically store a droplet's icon on the desktop, and you can drag images or folders to the icon to run the process.

Gamma

The brightness of the midtones in an image.

GIF

The Graphics Interchange Format, which holds up to 256 colors and uses lossless compression. The GIF format is typically best used for illustrations with flat color areas or images with transparency.

Grid

A set of evenly spaced vertical and horizontal guidelines that can help you position items accurately in an image.

Guide

A vertical or horizontal line to which items snap as you drag them. Guides are useful for aligning items on Web pages you design.

Hexadecimal color

The six-character code used in HTML to define a color. The first pair of characters represents the red component, the second pair represents green, and the third pair represents blue.

HTML

Hypertext Markup Language, used to code Web pages as text files. HTML tags are used to identify structural elements (such as headings, body text, lists, and tables), to create links to other files, to display images, and sometimes to indicate an element's appearance or position on the page.

ICC profile

A color management profile stored in the format devised by the International Color Consortium (ICC).

Interpolation

The method by which Photoshop resamples an image. Each interpolation method creates a different level of sharpness, accuracy, and processing speed.

JPEG

The Joint Photographic Experts Group image format, which can hold millions of colors and uses lossy compression. The JPEG format is typically best used for photographic images with no transparency.

Layer-based slice

A slice that automatically conforms to fit a layer's contents even if you resize or move the layer.

Link

Text or an image area that a Web-page viewer can click to jump to another page or to another area on the same page.

Linked slices

Slices that share optimization settings and that align dither patterns between adjacent slices.

Lossless compression

Compression that reduces an image's file size but retains all of its original data when decompressed and displayed.

Lossy compression

Compression that reduces an image's file size by discarding some of the data, thereby reducing image quality.

Matte color

A background color that either replaces transparent space in an image with no transparency, or acts as a blend color for semi-transparent pixels in an image with transparency.

Navbar

A navigation bar of buttons that link to pages within a Web site.

Non-lossy compression

See *Lossless compression.*

Optimization

Converting an image for the Web with the intent of creating the highest possible image quality and lowest possible file size.

Pixel dimensions

The width and height of an image as measured in pixels.

PNG

The Portable Network Graphics format, which uses lossless compression and supports transparency. The PNG-8 variant holds 256 colors and on/off transparency. The PNG-24 variant holds millions of colors and supports partial transparency.

Resampling

Changing the number of pixels in an image while retaining its basic appearance.

Resolution

The number of pixels per inch for a printed image, or the number of pixels in the horizontal and vertical dimensions of an image for the Web.

Sharpening

Applying a filter or tool that makes an image's edges appear clearer by adding to their contrast. Sharpening often improves clarity in images that have been downsampled for the Web.

Slicing

Dividing an image into a grid of smaller rectangular areas for the purpose of creating a large design without requiring one large download, and for creating effects such as navbar buttons.

Target (link)

A setting that specifies whether the link opens in the current browser window, for example, or in a new browser window.

Trimming

Eliminating excess pixels from an image's edges. Photoshop can automatically trim either fully transparent pixels or ones that match the top-left or bottom-right pixel color.

Tweening

Creating animation by automatically generating additional frames that blend between a starting and an ending frame.

Unsharp Mask

A sharpening filter that offers more control than the regular Sharpen filter.

Vector shape layer

A layer that consists of a color fill and a vector mask that defines a shape, hiding the color outside its borders.

Web photo gallery

A site whose primary purpose is to display images, typically with small thumbnail images linking to pages displaying larger versions of the images.

Web-safe color

One of the 216 colors that will be displayed correctly on either a Windows or Macintosh computer with an 8-bit (256-color maximum) video card.

Index

A

Actions
Creating, 4-8
Turning into droplets, 4-12
Alt text, assigning to slices, 3-2
Animations
Creating, 5-2
Saving in GIF format, 5-12
With motion blur, 5-9
With tweening, 5-6
Auto slices, 2-8

B

Badge icons, 2-8
Broadband connections, 1-2
Browser dithering, 4-3

C

Colors
And default color spaces, 4-2
Hexadecimal, 1-23
Matte, 1-11, 1-23
Web safe, 1-15
Compression
Lossy vs. non-lossy, 1-3
Weighted lossy, 1-20

D

Data sets
Creating for data-driven images, 4-22
Exporting as files, 4-26
Data-driven images, 4-18
Design considerations
Connection speeds, 1-2, 4-3
Monitor resolution, 2-2
Platforms, 4-2
Device Central, 3-6
Dithering, 1-15, 4-3
Downsampling, 1-5
Droplets
Creating from actions, 4-12
Defined, 4-8

E

Exporting
Animations, 5-12
Data sets as files, 4-26

High-resolution images with Zoomify, 3-12
Sliced images, 2-26

F

File size
Factors affecting, 1-3
Reducing through downsampling, 1-5
Reducing through trimming, 1-8
Target, 1-18
Filter, Unsharp Mask, 1-6

G

Gamma, Mac vs. Windows, 4-2
GIF format
Optimization options, 1-14
Saving animations in, 5-12
Transparency support, 1-21
Grids, showing and customizing, 2-4

H

Hexadecimal colors, 1-23
HTML
Designating image text as, 2-20
Formatting text with, 2-21
Generated for Web photo galleries, 4-15
Specifying file size with, 1-5

I

ICC profiles, 1-11
Image Processor script, 4-4
Image resolution, 1-5
Images
Creating for mobile devices, 3-6
Generating variations of through variables, 4-18
Interlaced GIFs, 1-15

J

JPEG format
And transparency, 1-21
Optimization options, 1-10

L

Layer-based slices, 2-8, 2-11
Link targets, 3-2
Linking slices, 2-16
Lossy compression, 1-3
Weighted, 1-20